Wonders of the Wild

SHARKS

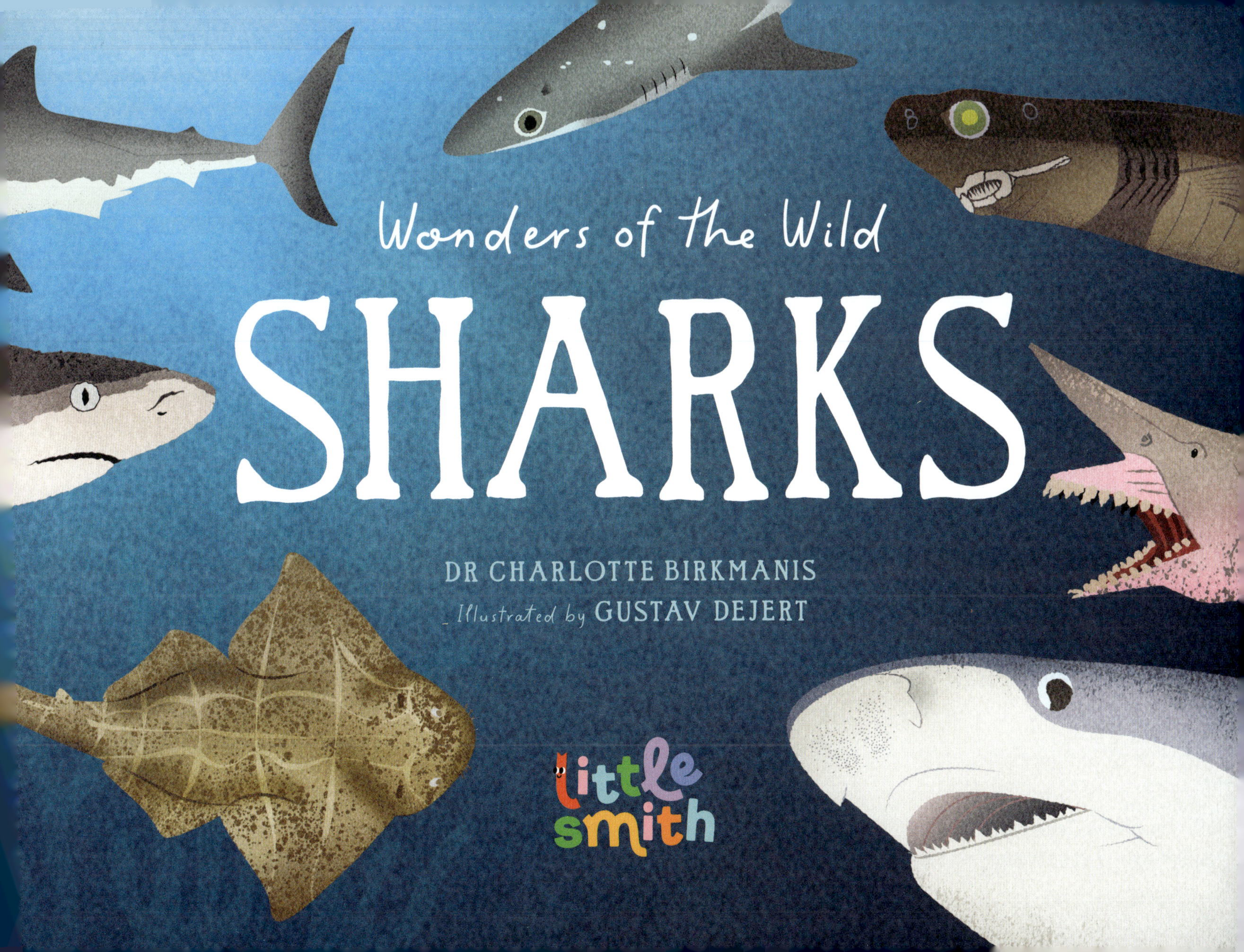

Wonders of the Wild

SHARKS

DR CHARLOTTE BIRKMANIS

Illustrated by GUSTAV DEJERT

little smith

Sharks are older than trees and the rings of Saturn!

Some fit in your hand while others are the size of a bus.

They come in pink, blue and even squirt luminous fluid at will! With more than 500 species, sharks fill a variety of ecosystem roles. They transport vital nutrients by eating in one area and pooping in another. As well as actively hunting prey, they keep populations healthy by eating the sick and the old. Just by being there, large sharks alter behaviour, creating a 'landscape of fear' which indirectly maintains coral reef and seagrass habitats. Sharks even help with climate change! By discouraging animals from overgrazing seagrass beds, seagrass can regenerate and function as carbon sinks. Sharks are ~15% carbon and at the end of their lives they sink, sequestering that carbon in the sea floor. Sharks need our help – but we need them too. We need a healthy ocean, and a healthy ocean needs sharks.

As you discover each new shark, you'll find definitions of words that appear in **bold** are defined in the glossary and anatomy pages.

The light shading on maps shows areas where a species is resident, and the darker shading shows where a species is possibly resident.

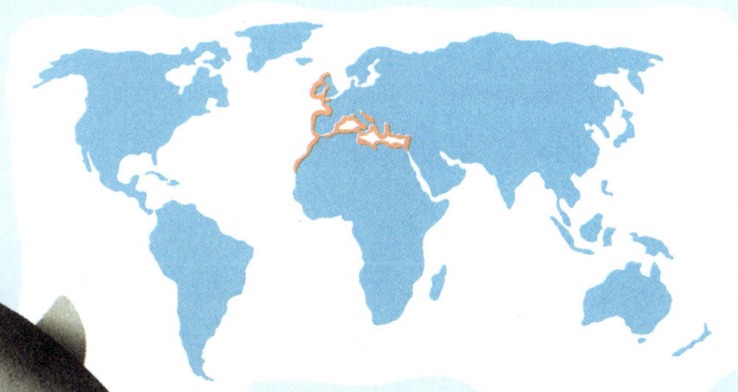

Anatomy

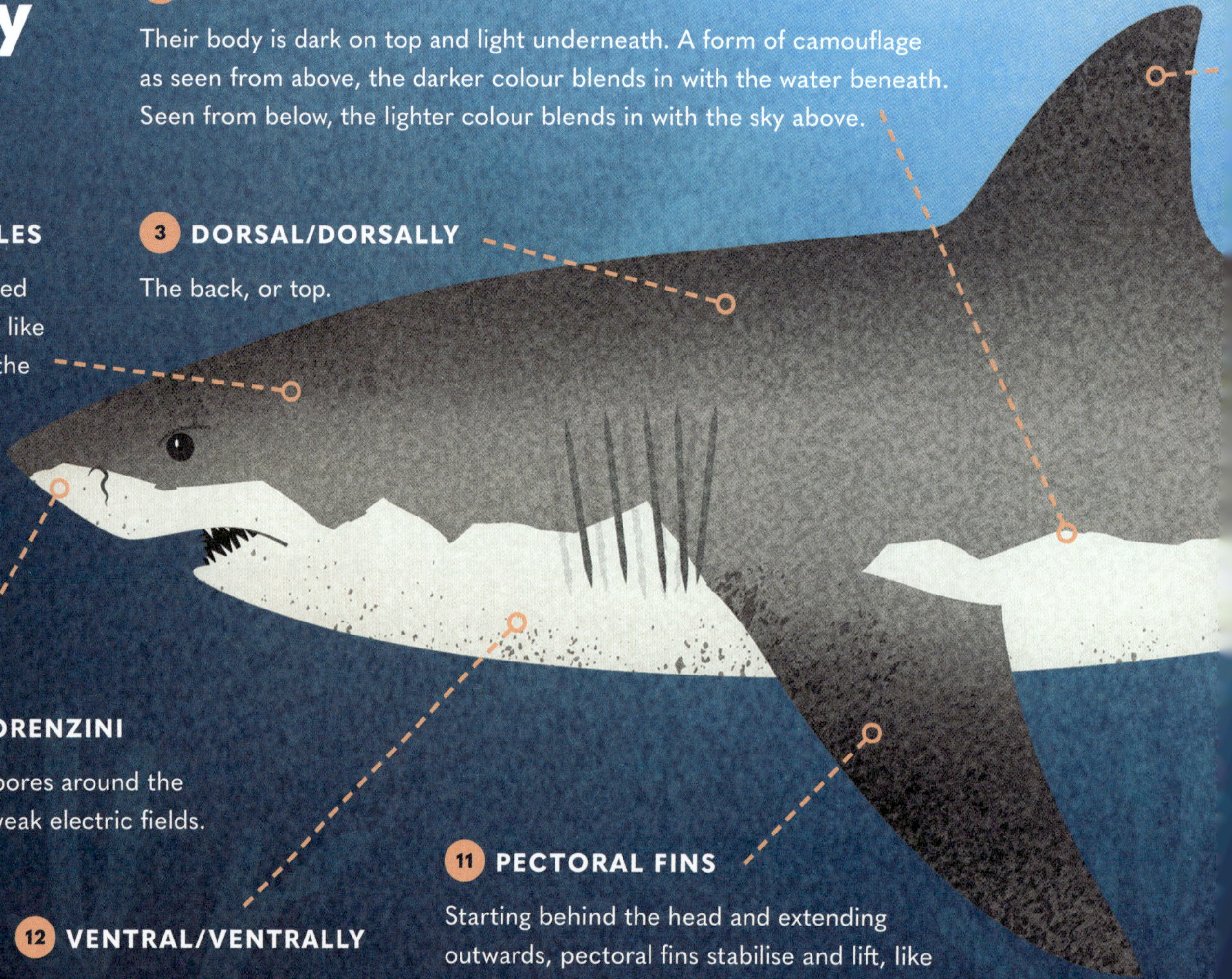

4 COUNTERSHADING

Their body is dark on top and light underneath. A form of camouflage as seen from above, the darker colour blends in with the water beneath. Seen from below, the lighter colour blends in with the sky above.

2 DERMAL DENTICLES

Tiny tooth-like scales buried in the skin that feel rough like sandpaper. They protect the shark and make them so streamlined that swimsuits for Olympians are made from fabric that mimics these 'skin teeth'.

3 DORSAL/DORSALLY

The back, or top.

1 AMPULLAE OF LORENZINI

Small, sensitive gel-filled pores around the shark's head that detect weak electric fields.

12 VENTRAL/VENTRALLY

The belly, or underneath.

11 PECTORAL FINS

Starting behind the head and extending outwards, pectoral fins stabilise and lift, like aeroplane wings. Larger in pelagic sharks.

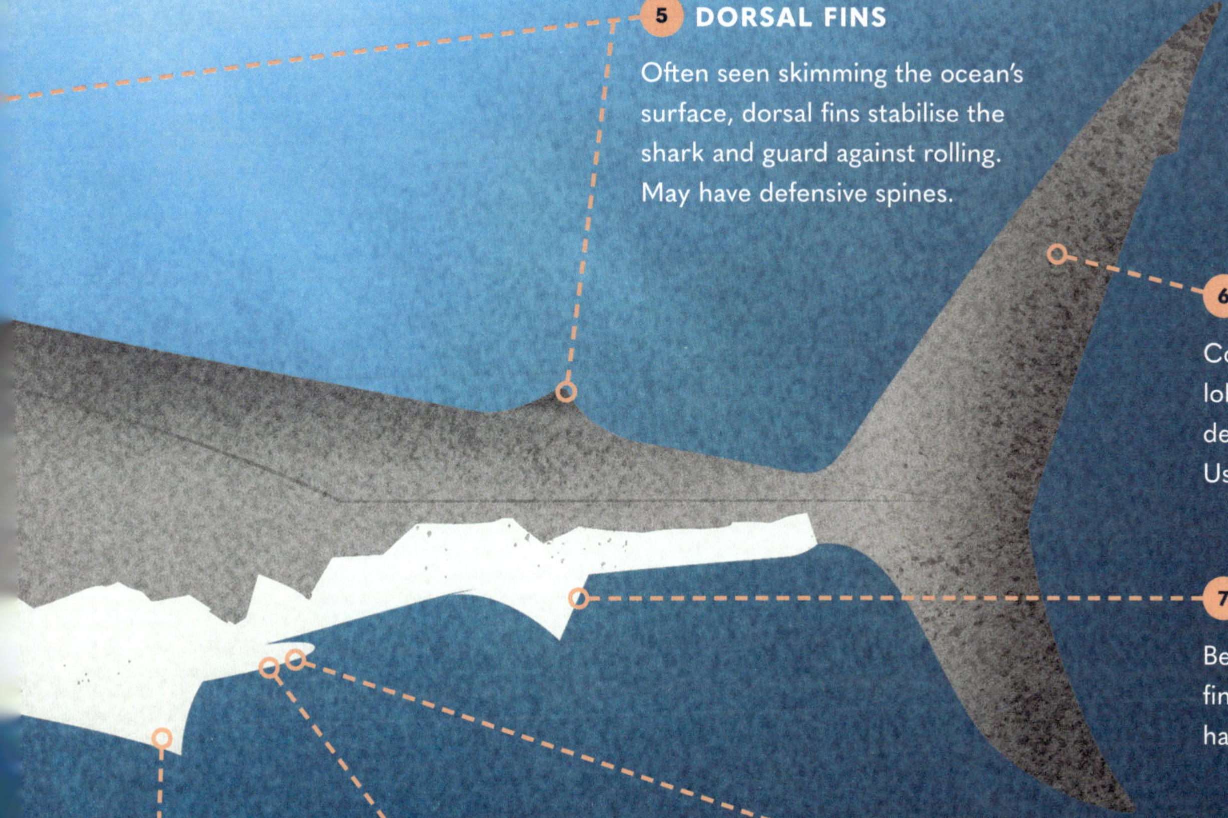

5 DORSAL FINS

Often seen skimming the ocean's surface, dorsal fins stabilise the shark and guard against rolling. May have defensive spines.

6 CAUDAL OR TAIL FINS

Consist of an upper and lower lobe of various sizes and shapes depending on the species. Usually provide propulsion.

7 ANAL FINS

Between the pelvic and caudal fins for stability. Not all sharks have them.

10 PELVIC FINS

Located towards the rear of the shark and are used to stabilise.

9 CLASPERS

Male sharks have paired claspers for reproduction on the inner margins of the pelvic fins. Female sharks do not have claspers.

8 CLOACA

The external opening of the digestive, urinary and genital tract.

Sharks need our help!

Sharks have roamed the oceans of our planet for millions of years. There are over 500 species of sharks – even more if you count their cartilaginous relatives, the rays, skates and chimaeras. A new species is found on average every two weeks.

You might think a world without sharks would be wonderful, but they control fish populations, consume sick individuals and preserve the delicate balance of marine ecosystems. A healthy ocean needs sharks and we need healthy oceans for food, jobs and even oxygen.

Although sharks are prey for crocodiles and even birds, the greatest threat to them is overfishing. Sharks are caught for their fins and their meat, and sometimes accidentally as bycatch. Other conservation challenges incude habitat destruction, climate change and pollution.

Sharks numbers are declining at a staggering rate. More than 70 per cent of the sharks that

once swam in the open ocean are now gone and over one-third of shark species and their relatives are at risk of extinction.

It doesn't help that sharks are generally slow-growing and mature relatively late in life. Some species only produce a handful of babies – called pups – every few years and their pregnancies can last for more than a year! All this makes it difficult for shark populations to recover.

But you can help. Choose your favourite species and go out on a boat to see them in the ocean. Do a snorkel tour on your next holiday to discover the wonders of the wild for yourself. By supporting regenerative tourism, scientific research and responsible fishing practices, as well as making sustainable seafood choices, you can play your part in keeping our oceans healthy and making sure that sharks will always be the guardians of our oceans.

Glossary

BENTHIC

An animal that lives on the ocean floor.

BIOLUMINESCENCE

Light produced by living organisms.

CONSERVATION STATUS

The extinction risk of a species based on the IUCN's Red List of Threatened Species. The categories are Extinct, Extinct in the Wild, Critically Endangered, Endangered, Vulnerable, Near Threatened, Least Concern, Data Deficient and Not Evaluated.

ENDEMIC

Restricted to a certain location.

INTERTIDAL ZONE

The area where the ocean meets the land between high and low tides.

LECITHOTROPHIC

An embryo that relies solely on their egg yolk for nutrition.

MESOPELAGIC ZONE

The ocean between 200 m and 1,000 m (660–3,280 ft) below the surface.

OVIPAROUS

An animal that lays eggs that hatch outside the mother.

OVOVIVIPAROUS

An animal that produces eggs that develop and hatch inside the mother who then gives birth to live young.

PELAGIC

Relating to the open ocean.

SPIRACLES

A pair of openings behind the eyes that act like snorkels. They allow the shark to breathe, even when buried in the sand.

BIGEYE THRESHER

ALOPIAS SUPERCILIOSUS

HABITAT

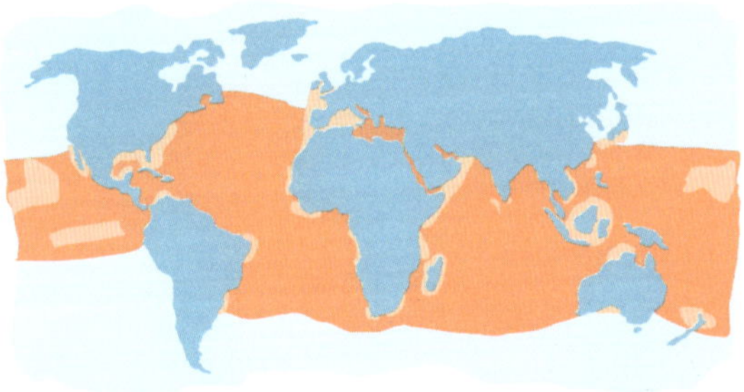

Bigeye thresher sharks are highly migratory, dwelling in tropical and temperate oceans across the planet. They sometimes swim in shallow coastal waters but they are usually found in the high seas.

DIET

The diet of these extraordinary sharks consists of squid and fish, such as small billfish, herring, mackerel and hake.

BIOLOGY

- All three thresher shark species have distinctive tails. Bigeye threshers have an enormously elongated upper lobe – which can be as long as the rest of the shark. They are a beautiful metallic purple to brown-grey.
- Bigeye threshers are named for their huge eyes, which rotate upward, making them look cute, but worried. Their eyes can be 10 cm (4 in) in diameter and are built for the low light conditions of the deep ocean. These sharks spend their days deep in the ocean and their nights hunting near the surface.
- All thresher sharks have a special blood circulatory system that keeps them warm even when they are swimming in cold, deep waters.

CONSERVATION STATUS

Vulnerable

MAXIMUM SIZE

4.8 m (15.7 ft)

FIN FACT

Uses a whiplike action of its long tail to stun its prey!

BLACKTIP REEF SHARK

CARCHARHINUS MELANOPTERUS

HABITAT

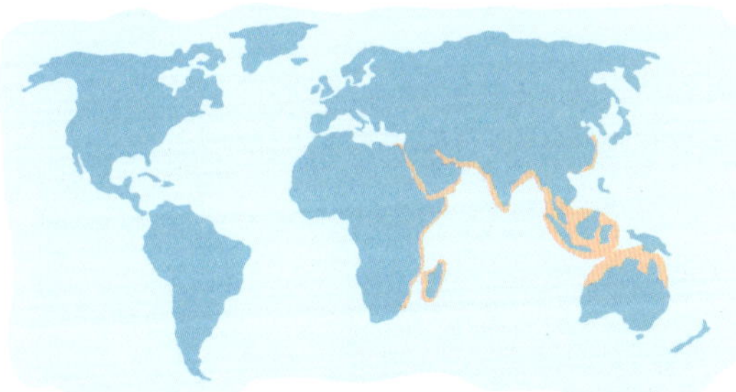

You've probably seen these sharks in an aquarium or while snorkelling. They swim in tropical waters of the Indian and Pacific oceans and even in the Mediterranean Sea. They dwell in and around coral reefs and can be found from the surface down to at least 75 m (246 ft). The pups can also live in mangrove forests.

DIET

These sharks eat fish such as mullet, crustaceans, molluscs and even land and sea snakes.

BIOLOGY

- These easily identifiable sharks are named for the distinct black tips on their first **dorsal fin** and lower **caudal fin** lobes. Yellow-brown to grey above, with white **countershading** below, they have a conspicuous white band along the flank (side) and prominent black tips on all fins.
- Like most sharks, blacktip reef sharks sport a sheath of **dermal denticles** all over their bodies, which help them stay streamlined when swimming and protected from parasites.
- Blacktip reef sharks cooperate and hunt as a team. Groups of them herd schools of fish around coral.

CONSERVATION STATUS

Vulnerable

MAXIMUM SIZE

2 m (6.5 ft)

FIN FACT

Has long-term friends, choosing to spend time with some individuals and avoid others!

CROCODILE SHARK

PSEUDOCARCHARIAS KAMOHARAI

HABITAT

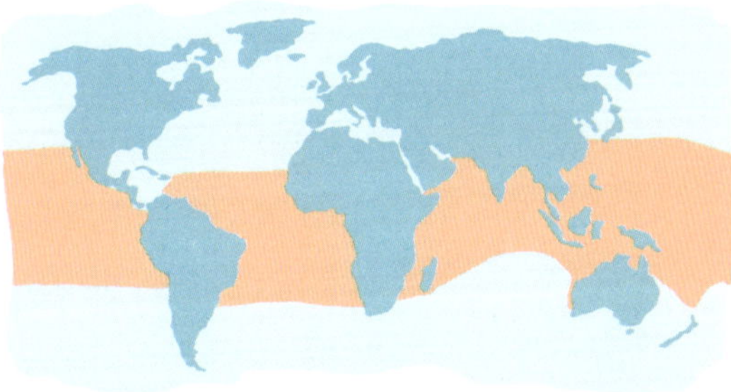

These **mesopelagic** sharks live in the tropical and subtropical waters of the Indian, Pacific and Atlantic oceans. During the day, they swim down to depths of at least 590 m (1,940 ft), but more commonly around 200 m (660 ft), and migrate to the surface at night.

DIET

Carnivorous crocodile sharks feast on small bony fish, shrimp and squid.

BIOLOGY

- These spindle-shaped sharks have very large eyes with small low **dorsal fins**. Crocodile sharks are light or dark grey above and pale below, with fins edged in white. They sometimes have small white spots on their body.
- Their large eyes suggest that they are nocturnal hunters that use sight to pick out the silhouettes of their prey or glowing **bioluminescence**.
- To date, crocodile sharks are poorly studied – we don't know much about their biology.

CONSERVATION STATUS

Least Concern

MAXIMUM SIZE

1.2 m (4 ft)

FIN FACT

Its large liver makes up about 20% of its total weight!

PORT JACKSON SHARK

HETERODONTUS PORTUSJACKSONI

HABITAT

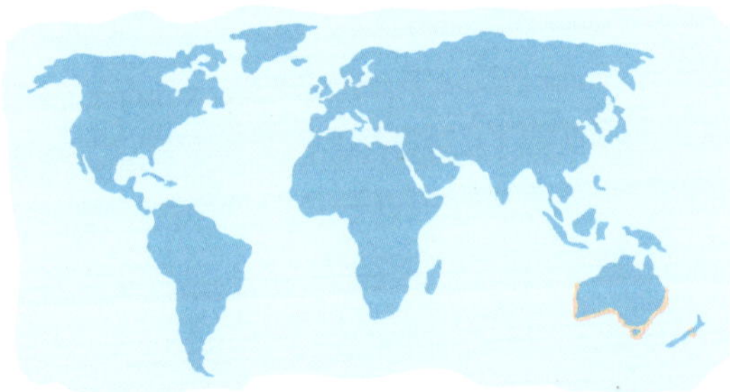

Port Jackson sharks are found off the southern coast of Australia. When inshore, this shark prefers to rest in caves with sandy floors and in open trenches of shallow rocky reefs. Almost all sharks in the area rest in just a few sites.

DIET

These nocturnal sharks feed on **benthic** invertebrates, such as sea urchins and starfish, as well as molluscs and crustaceans. They also occasionally eat rubbish, such as mammal fur and orange peel.

BIOLOGY

- Port Jackson sharks are very distinctive. They have dark bands over the eyes and harness-like markings across the back. They also have a blunt head with prominent crests above their eyes and a spine on both **dorsal fins**.
- Unlike the shark teeth you probably imagine, the teeth of Port Jackson sharks aren't serrated. They eat a lot of hard-shelled prey, so they need to hold, break, crush and grind their food. Their front teeth are small and pointed, while their back teeth are broad and flat.
- Juvenile Port Jackson sharks have smaller, more pointed teeth and dig up food by sucking in sand then blowing it out of their gill covers.

CONSERVATION STATUS

Least Concern

MAXIMUM SIZE

1.6 m (5 ft)

FIN FACT

Navigates a maze faster when with a trained buddy, showing that they learn from peers!

WHALE SHARK

RHINCODON TYPUS

HABITAT

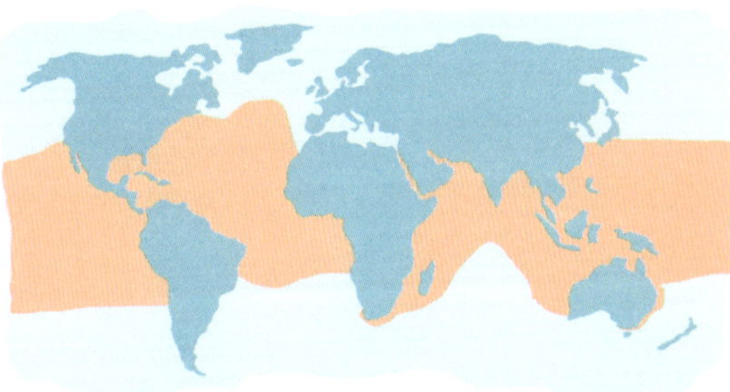

Whale sharks are found alone, or in groups called aggregations of over 100 sharks. They are highly migratory, crossing oceans to return to the same sites every year.

DIET

Whale sharks are often vertical, their heads at or near the surface, feeding on tiny planktonic and nektonic species, such as anchovies, tuna, squid and crustaceans. When feeding, they turn their head from side to side and gape up to 28 times a minute to suck in all the tiny animals.

BIOLOGY

- These gentle giants are not only the world's largest sharks, but the largest living fish on the planet.
- The unique spots and stripes on their skin are like our fingerprints. Computer software that was designed to map the stars is used to identify individual whale sharks from their unique pattern.
- Whale sharks give birth to up to 300 fully developed live pups about 40 cm (16 in) long.

CONSERVATION STATUS

Endangered

MAXIMUM SIZE

20 m (66 ft)

FIN FACT

They can retract their tiny teeth-covered eyeballs into their eye sockets for protection!

SPEARTOOTH SHARK

GLYPHIS GLYPHIS

HABITAT

These sharks are thought to dwell in tidal rivers, river mouths and coastal waters across northern Australia and southern New Guinea. Unlike bull sharks, speartooth sharks stay in the salty, muddy waters of tidal rivers, with juveniles and adolescents found in murky tropical tidal rivers.

DIET

Based on their slender teeth, these sharks likely eat fish and crustaceans. Their small eyes and abundant sensory **ampullae** suggest they rely on electromagnetic receptors to hunt.

BIOLOGY

- As very few adults have been caught or seen, these sharks are mysterious – virtually nothing is known about their biology, where they live or give birth.
- They are slate-grey **dorsally** and white **ventrally**, with an identifying 'watermark' where the colour changes abruptly just below the eyes. They have a short and broadly rounded snout, small eyes and relatively few teeth – 54 rows in both jaws.
- Female speartooth sharks stay in the same river while males move between rivers that can be up to 150 km (93 miles) apart.

CONSERVATION STATUS

Vulnerable

MAXIMUM SIZE

Unknown, but perhaps 3 m (10 ft)

FIN FACT

There are only 2,500 to 10,000 mature speartooth sharks worldwide.

BROWNBANDED BAMBOO SHARK

CHILOSCYLLIUM PUNCTATUM

HABITAT

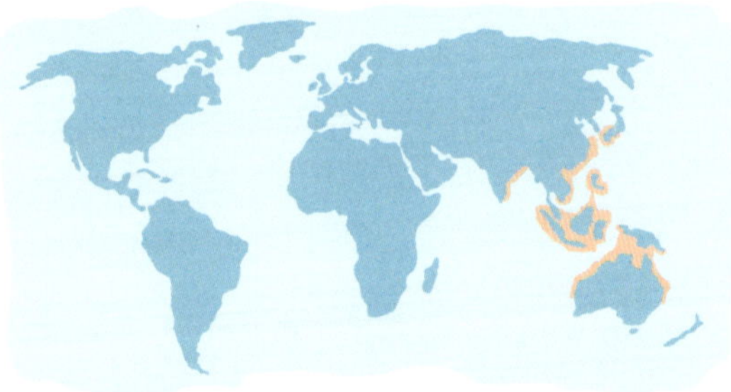

These sharks live in a variety of habitats, including coral reefs and tidepools. They are widely found in the tropical and warm-temperate waters of the Indian and western Pacific oceans.

DIET

They hunt at night for **benthic** animals, including small fish, worms and invertebrates.

BIOLOGY

- Brownbanded bamboo sharks are known as 'cat sharks', because their nasal barbels (sensory organs for locating food hidden in the sand) resemble the whiskers of a cat.
- They are **oviparous** – they lay elongated, flattened eggs (often called a 'mermaid's purse'). From inside their leathery egg case, the embryos can detect predators and freeze or even stop breathing to avoid being discovered.
- The embryos hatch when they are 13–18 cm (5–7 in) long and then quickly swim away. The pups have a distinctive, high-contrast banding pattern that mimics poisonous animals, such as sea snakes, to help them evade predators. This is known as Batesian mimicry.

CONSERVATION STATUS

Near Threatened

MAXIMUM SIZE

1.3 m (4 ft)

FIN FACT

Can survive out of water for up to 12 hours!

GREENLAND SHARK

SOMNIOSUS MICROCEPHALUS

HABITAT

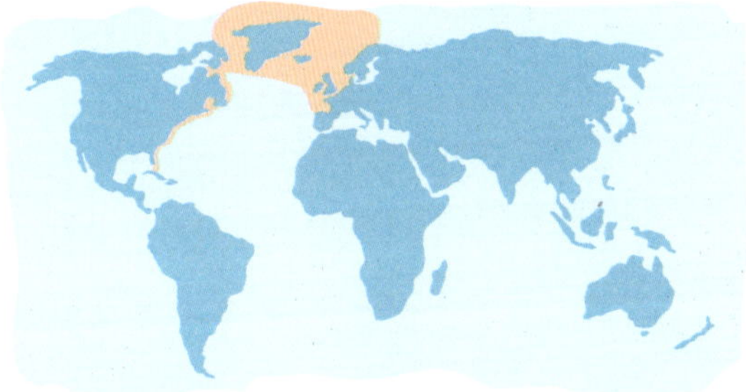

Greenland sharks mostly live in the cold Arctic and north Atlantic oceans. Although occasionally found in shallow waters, they mainly occur in waters from 200 m to almost 3,000 m (660–9,800 ft).

DIET

These seemingly slow-moving sharks manage to capture much faster prey, such as reindeer, seabirds and even polar bears, but it is not clear if this food is scavenged when already dead or actively hunted.

BIOLOGY

- Like great white sharks, Greenland sharks are large and carnivorous – but they couldn't be more different. These sluggish sharks have a small head, short snout and tiny eyes at the front of a thickset, cylindrical body.
- Greenland sharks often have a parasite on their eyes, which destroys the corneal tissue and makes the shark partially blind.
- They swim in groups or pairs, 2.8 m (9 ft) apart, at an average speed of less than 2 km/h (1.2 mph).
- Greenland sharks are the only sharks that can tolerate freezing waters all year round, as they produce a natural antifreeze.

CONSERVATION STATUS

Vulnerable

MAXIMUM SIZE

6.4 m (possibly 7.3 m) (21–24 ft)

FIN FACT

Can live for 500 years – females don't mature until they are over 150 years old!

BLUNTNOSE SIXGILL SHARK

HABITAT

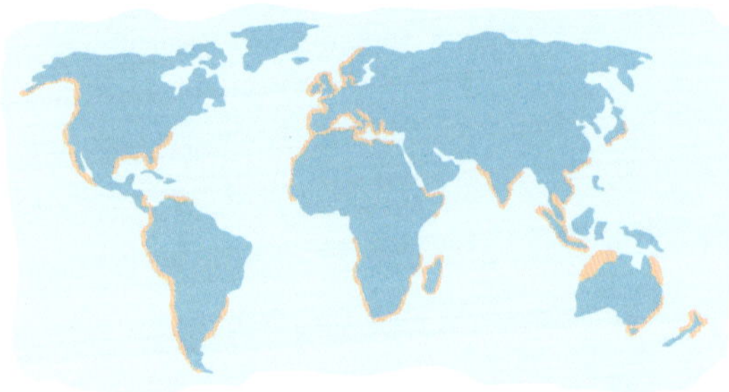

These sharks have a patchy range across all the oceans, mostly found at depths of 200–1,100 m (660–3,600 ft). How deep they live depends on their age and the water temperature. Juveniles tend to live in shallow waters in colder areas closer to Earth's poles.

DIET

Found on the sea floor by day, these sharks move to the surface at night to feed on a wide range of prey, such as other sharks, rays, chimaeras, fish, squid, shrimp, crabs and seals.

BIOLOGY

- Most sharks have five gills and two **dorsal fins**, but these broad-headed, heavy-bodied sharks have six gills and one **dorsal fin**! They are aptly named for their blunt, rounded snout and six long gill slits.
- We don't know a lot about these slow, strong swimmers, but they live in the deep ocean and are often seen alone. We do know that it closely resembles Triassic fossils that are approximately 200 million years old.
- Females mature at lengths of 3.5–4.2 m (11–14 ft) and males mature at 3.1–3.3 m (10–11 ft). Pups are born at 74 cm (2.4 ft).

CONSERVATION STATUS

Near Threatened

MAXIMUM SIZE

5.5 m (18 ft)

FIN FACT

Has large, teardrop-shaped, fluorescent green eyes.

ANGULAR ROUGHSHARK

HABITAT

These rare sharks live at depths between 35 m and 1,300 m (115–4,300 ft) in the Atlantic Ocean from Norway to South Africa, and in the Mediterranean Sea. There are records of angular roughsharks from Mozambique, but these may be a different species.

DIET

Angular roughsharks are suction feeders that eat **benthic** animals such as worms, crustaceans, molluscs, small fish and even the eggs of other sharks and rays.

BIOLOGY

- These bizarre-looking sharks are grey to grey-brown with unmistakable high bodies and bristly textured skin. Their bodies are triangular in cross-section, with a broad, flattened head, blunt and flat snout and two relatively large sail-like **dorsal fins** with a spine.
- The males mature at around 60 cm (24 in) and females around 65 cm (26 in). Females give birth to 7 to 23 pups in a litter, each 21–24 cm (8–9 in) long.
- Although angular roughsharks can grow to 1.5 m (5 ft), most are less than 1 m (3 ft) in length.

CONSERVATION STATUS

Endangered

MAXIMUM SIZE

1.5 m (5 ft)

FIN FACT

It stops and hovers over the sea floor, then uses its fins to move forward.

LEMON SHARK

NEGAPRION BREVIROSTRIS

HABITAT

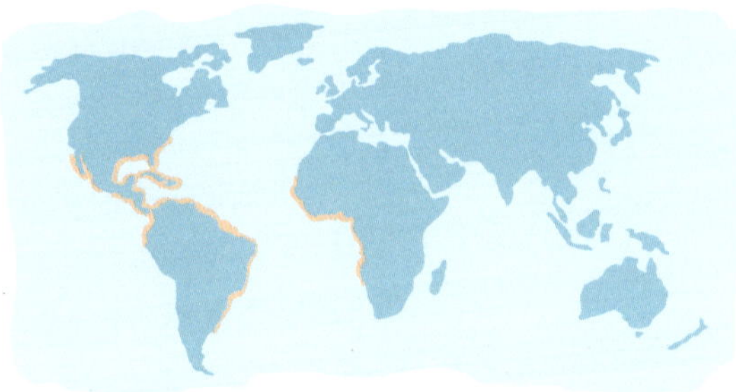

Lemon sharks occur in coastal tropical and subtropical waters of the Atlantic and eastern Pacific oceans. They usually live in shallow water, and the juveniles spend time in mangrove habitats – perfect for hiding from roving predators and finding food.

DIET

These sharks eat bony fish, crustaceans (crabs), molluscs (octopus) and stingrays, but also prey on seabirds and smaller sharks – even other lemon sharks!

BIOLOGY

- Lemon sharks are named for the yellow hue of their skin, which provides camouflage against the sandy sea floor.
- There are two species of lemon sharks. The sharptooth lemon shark (*Negaprion acutidens*) is an Endangered species found in coastal tropical and subtropical waters of the Indian and Pacific oceans.
- Lemon sharks are very social and prefer to be in groups with others of the same size. They form and maintain social networks, preferring to spend time with specific individuals or 'friends'. They also have distinct personalities – some are bolder than others.

CONSERVATION STATUS

Vulnerable

MAXIMUM SIZE

3.4 m (11 ft)

FIN FACT

Learns by watching other lemon sharks perform tasks.

PACIFIC SLEEPER SHARK

SOMNIOSUS PACIFICUS

HABITAT

These deepwater sharks are found in the north Pacific Ocean and Arctic Ocean, from the surface to more than 2,200 m (7,200 ft) deep. In cold surface waters, they range into the **intertidal zone**, but dwell deeper and never visit the surface in warmer temperate waters.

DIET

These elusive sharks feed on fish, octopus, squid and crabs, as well as seals and dead animals.

BIOLOGY

- These rarely seen sharks live in the deep ocean. Some sharks spend their days in the ocean depths, and then migrate up to swim near the surface of the water at night.
- Females mature at 3.65 m (12 ft) and males at 3.85 m (13 ft) long. The pups are thought to measure 40 cm (16 in) long at birth.
- The meat of Pacific sleeper sharks contains a toxin that produces symptoms of drunkenness when eaten.

CONSERVATION STATUS

Near Threatened

MAXIMUM SIZE

7 m (23 ft)

FIN FACT

One was found inside the caldera of an underwater volcano near the Solomon Islands!

SPINNER SHARK

CARCHARHINUS BREVIPINNA

HABITAT

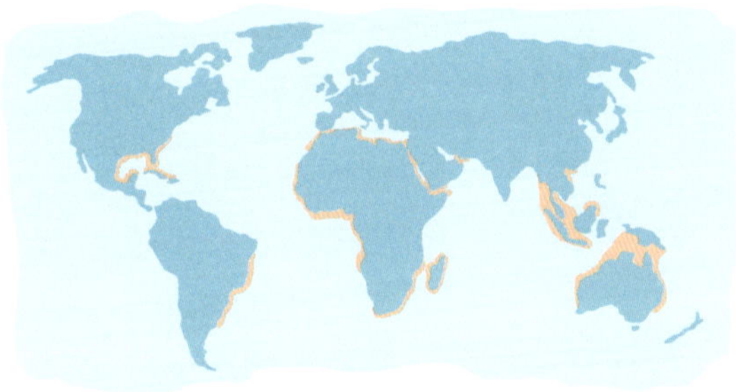

These sensational sharks swim in tropical and warm temperate waters of the Mediterranean Sea and the Atlantic, Indian and western Pacific oceans. They occur both inshore and offshore on continental shelves from the surface to 200 m (660 ft).

DIET

These sharks mainly eat **pelagic** bony fish, but also small sharks, squid, cuttlefish and octopus.

BIOLOGY

- Spinner sharks are aptly named for their distinctive spinning behaviour when feeding. They swim through schools of bait fish, spinning and snapping at fish as they zoom upwards. Then they breach the surface of the ocean and spin in the air.
- These highly migratory sharks form large schools that are often seen inshore, and have nursery grounds in shallow, near-shore waters.
- The lifespan of spinner sharks depends on where they live. In Australian waters, females mature at 8.5 years and live for 31 years, but in the Gulf of Mexico, females take just 7.6 years to mature and have a maximum age of 17.5 years.

CONSERVATION STATUS

Vulnerable

MAXIMUM SIZE

3 m (10 ft)

FIN FACT

Performs spectacular aerial acrobatics, making vertical spinning leaps almost 3 m (10 ft) high!

HORN SHARK

HETERODONTUS FRANCISCI

HABITAT

Horn sharks are found in eastern Pacific Ocean waters over 21°C (70°F) of the US and Mexican coasts, and possibly Ecuador and Peru. Adolescents live in deeper water, while juveniles live on the sandy bottom and use feeding pits made by rays for shelter. Adults inhabit rocky reefs with crevices and caves, or algae cover.

DIET

Horn sharks eat crabs, fish and sea urchins – adults often eat enough sea urchin to turn their teeth purple!

BIOLOGY

- Horn sharks are named after the sharp spines that are present in front of both **dorsal fins**.
- Slow and sporadic swimmers, they blend in with the greens and browns of their habitat. These small, elusive sharks hunt at night and by day, hide in caves, under ledges or among kelp.
- Horn sharks divide themselves into different areas according to size and maturity, to prevent competition. Adults that live on reefs have shorter fin spines than those living in algae, as their spines get worn down by going in and out of caves.

CONSERVATION STATUS

Least Concern

MAXIMUM SIZE

1.2 m (4 ft)

FIN FACT

Returns to the same resting place at dawn and stays there until evening.

GREAT WHITE SHARK

CARCHARODON CARCHARIAS

HABITAT

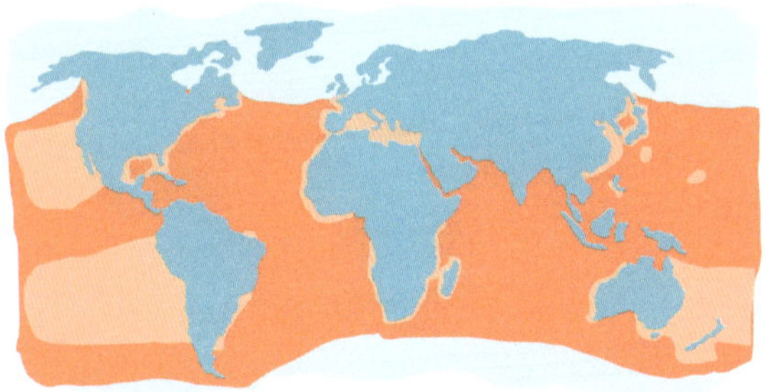

Great white sharks live in waters that are between 12°C and 24°C (54–75°F) and less than 205 m (670 ft) deep, both along the coast and in the open ocean. They can dive to depths of 1,200 m (3,900 ft). They usually travel alone or in pairs, rather than in a school, but may feed in groups of 10 or more.

DIET

Young great white sharks feed on fish, squid and stingrays. Adults feast on large fish, other sharks, sea turtles and marine mammals.

BIOLOGY

- Great white sharks are large and torpedo-shaped with a pointed snout and large fins. Like most sharks, they have **countershading** – dark grey or bronze on top and white underneath.
- These sharks are **ovoviviparous** – they give birth to 2 to 17 fully developed pups that hatch from eggs inside the mother's body.
- Great white sharks can live for up to 73 years. Females mature at 33 years of age.

CONSERVATION STATUS

Vulnerable

MAXIMUM SIZE

6.4 m (21 ft)

FIN FACT

Keeps its body temperature warmer than the water it is swimming in.

LEOPARD SHARK

TRIAKIS SEMIFASCIATA

HABITAT

Leopard sharks are common on the sandy bottoms of bays or estuaries along the coast of the eastern Pacific Ocean, from Washington, USA, to Mazatlán, Mexico.

DIET

These sharks skim the sea floor to catch crustaceans, such as crabs and shrimp, bony fish and their eggs, and burrowing worms. As they age, they dine on more fish and fewer crabs – sometimes even other sharks.

BIOLOGY

- Leopard sharks have a broad, short snout and distinctive black saddle marks on their silver or bronze-grey back and sides.
- Although they can travel long distances through deep water relatively rapidly (105 km or 65 miles in a week), they don't tend to stay in the same area.
- Leopard sharks live for at least 25 years. The females reach maturity between 10 and 15 years of age, and the males mature between 7 and 13 years.

CONSERVATION STATUS

Least Concern

MAXIMUM SIZE

2 m (6.5 ft)

FIN FACT

A pregnant female stays in shallow warm water to speed up the development of her embryos.

NINJA LANTERNSHARK

ETMOPTERUS BENCHLEYI

HABITAT

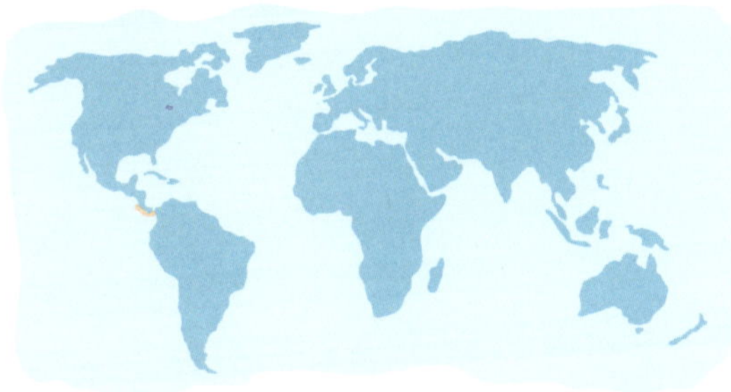

This newly discovered species of shark dwells in the ocean depths from 836 m to 1,443 m (2,740–4,730 ft), in the eastern central Pacific Ocean, from Nicaragua to Panama. Larger adults swim deeper than smaller, immature ninja lanternsharks.

DIET

The diet of these deep-sea ninjas is unknown, but they probably dine on small fish.

BIOLOGY

- This species is officially named after Peter Benchley, the author of *Jaws*. As their entire body is black, the young cousin of the scientist who found it suggested the common name 'ninja'.
- They have a cloaking device – **bioluminescent** photophores on their belly blend in with the little light that reaches the depths of the oceans, making them invisible from below. A win–win, allowing them to both avoid becoming lunch and find a tasty snack.
- These unique sharks are covered in slender, short, hook-like **dermal denticles** and their fins have thin, translucent margins.

CONSERVATION STATUS

Least Concern

MAXIMUM SIZE

52 cm (20 in)

FIN FACT

In the deep, dark ocean Ninja lanternsharks glow!

GREAT HAMMERHEAD SHARK

HABITAT

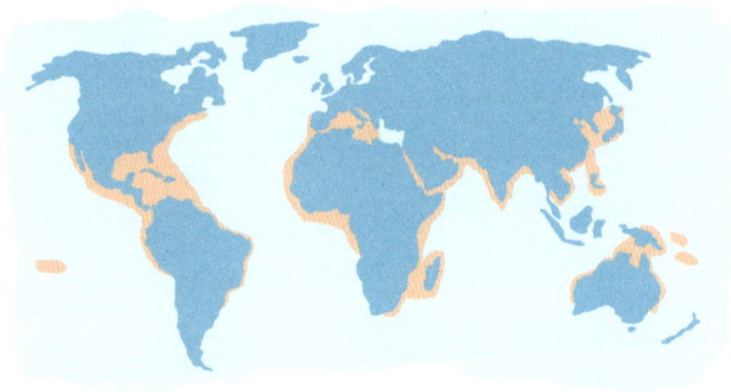

Great hammerhead sharks are found both far offshore and in shallow coastal areas and lagoons. They swim to depths of 300 m (980 ft) but are usually found in the top 100 m (330 ft) of tropical and warm temperate seas.

DIET

These wide-ranging sharks feed on stingrays, groupers and sea catfish, but they also eat other small bony fish, sharks (even other great hammerheads), squid, crabs and lobsters.

BIOLOGY

- This is the largest of the three hammerhead species. They have a distinctive notch at the front and centre of their 'hammer head' (cephalofoil) and a very large first **dorsal fin**.
- We don't know how many great hammerheads swim in our oceans, but we know they can live for up to 44 years.
- These sharks swim solo and migrate long distances – 1,200 km (750 miles) or more. There is likely to be a nursery area for young sharks in the Atlantic Ocean, off the US coast.

CONSERVATION STATUS

Critically Endangered

MAXIMUM SIZE

6.1 m (20 ft)

FIN FACT

Hammerheads can be skittish and are often scared of divers' bubbles.

ATLANTIC NURSE SHARK

GINGLYMOSTOMA CIRRATUM

HABITAT

Atlantic nurse sharks swim in the warm waters of the Atlantic Ocean, from the USA to Brazil, and Morocco to Angola. Commonly found among seagrasses, reefs, sandflats and mangroves, they have small home ranges and are found at depths to 130 m (430 ft).

DIET

These sharks dine on small fish that would be too fast to catch during the day but rest at night, along with shrimp, crabs, lobsters, octopus, sea urchins and stingrays.

BIOLOGY

- The teeth of these sharks do not overlap, so new teeth can move forward in the jaw without being blocked. Pups replace their teeth quicker than adults, and teeth are replaced faster in warmer waters.
- During courtship, a male approaches a female and bites one of her **pectoral fins** while trying to turn her onto one side to mate. To avoid being bitten, females sometimes swim in very shallow water so they can bury their pectoral fins in the sand.
- These nocturnal sharks use powerful throat muscles to suck up food with tremendous speed.

CONSERVATION STATUS

Vulnerable

MAXIMUM SIZE

4.3 m (14 ft)

FIN FACT

Preys on large snails by flipping the shell over and sucking out the snail!

COOKIECUTTER SHARK

HABITAT

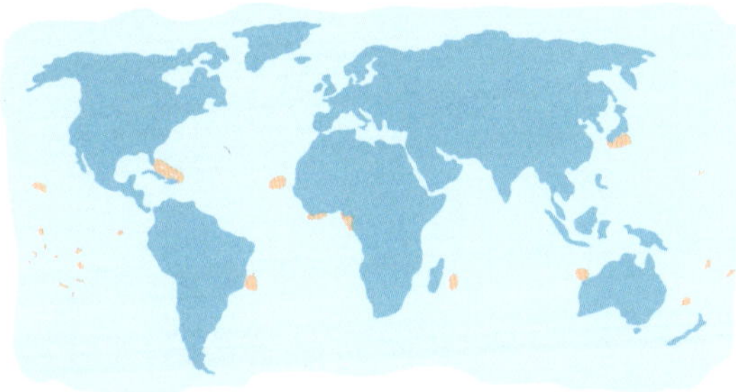

These deep-sea sharks are found in tropical and temperate oceans. They live in schools from the surface down to 3,700 m (12,100 ft) spending their days in the depths and coming up to the surface waters at night.

DIET

They feed on squid, fish and marine mammals that are much larger than they are. They attach to prey using a specialised jaw to form a vacuum, then spin their body to cut out a plug of flesh, swallowing the meal before detaching.

BIOLOGY

- Cookiecutter sharks are small and cigar-shaped, with a dark band around their gills like a necklace. They are dark brown on top, but have photophores that give their lighter underside a greenish glow.
- They are **ovoviviparous** – giving birth to 6 to 12 fully developed pups that hatch from eggs inside the mother's body.
- They shed all their teeth at once and eat the bottom ones. The upper teeth are small and slender, like thorns, and the lower teeth are large and flat, like triangles.

CONSERVATION STATUS

Least Concern

MAXIMUM SIZE

56 cm (22 in)

FIN FACT

The common name comes from the circular cookie-shaped wounds it leaves on its prey.

PORBEAGLE SHARK

HABITAT

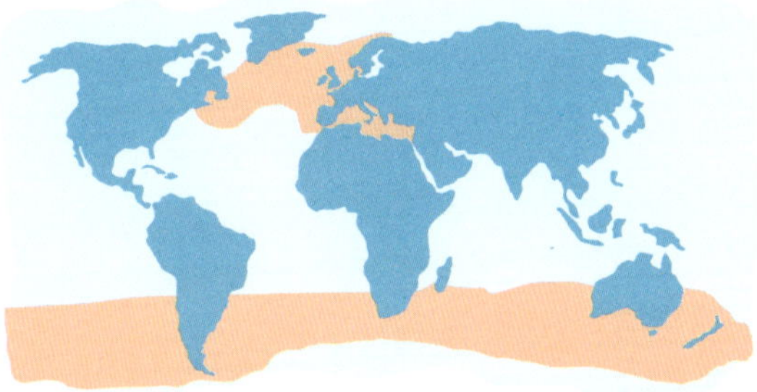

Porbeagles swim in coastal and open waters below 18°C (64°F), from the surface to depths of over 1,800 m (5,900 ft) in the north Atlantic Ocean in the Northern Hemisphere and in a band of temperate and cold-temperate water in the Southern Hemisphere.

DIET

The diet of playful porbeagles changes as they grow. Young sharks mainly consume cephalopods such as squid, and shift to eating fish, such as mackerel, when mature.

BIOLOGY

- With a heavy spindle-shaped body, conspicuous white rear tip on the first **dorsal fin** and a tiny, pivoting second dorsal fin, porbeagles can be found swimming alone, in schools and in feeding clusters grouped by sex and size – possibly to stop cannibalism by adult males.
- We don't know how many porbeagle sharks there are, but we do know that there are separate subpopulations. They live for up to 65 years, migrating more than 2,300 km (1,430 miles).
- They are uterine cannibals, feeding on unfertilised eggs in the womb after their own yolk sac is absorbed.

CONSERVATION STATUS

Vulnerable

MAXIMUM SIZE

3.6 m (12 ft)

FIN FACT

Tolerates water temperatures from –1°C to 23°C (30–73°F).

WHITETIP REEF SHARK

TRIAENODON OBESUS

HABITAT

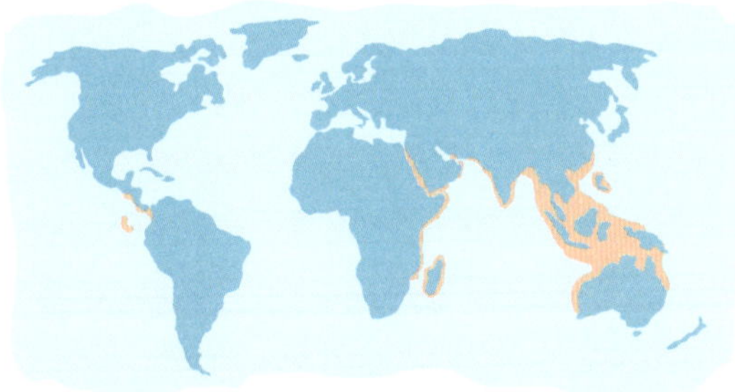

These widespread sharks occur on coral reefs in the clear tropical waters of the Indian and Pacific oceans. They spend their days in large groups, lying on sandy bottoms, under ledges or in caves, staying in one cave for weeks!

DIET

The nocturnal whitetip reef shark eats reef fish, such as snapper, triggerfish and parrotfish, octopus, spiny lobsters and crabs.

BIOLOGY

- Whitetip reef sharks are named for the brilliant white tips on the first **dorsal fin** and upper **caudal fin**. They are slender sharks with oval eyes and a short, blunt snout, brownish grey on top and whitish underneath.
- Unlike many sharks, whitetip reef sharks don't need to keep swimming to breathe, so they pile on top of each other and can stay motionless for hours.
- Whitetip reef sharks wedge their slim flexible bodies and snouts into hidden reef crevices to catch their prey. Other sharks take advantage of this – grey reef sharks often follow foraging whitetip reef sharks to catch the fish they flush out.

CONSERVATION STATUS

Vulnerable

MAXIMUM SIZE

2.1 m (7 ft)

FIN FACT

This homebody travels less than 600 m (1,970 ft) a year.

SALMON SHARK

LAMNA DITROPIS

HABITAT

These speedy sharks are only found in the northern Pacific Ocean, where they swim in cool waters, both near the shore and in the open ocean to depths of 1,800 m (5,900 ft).

DIET

Salmon sharks are named after their favourite snack, Pacific salmon, but they also eat other fish such as herring, sardines, lanternfish, spiny dogfish and squid – even sea otters and birds! Salmon sharks may dine alone or with up to 40 other sharks.

BIOLOGY

- Salmon sharks resemble their close relative the great white shark, except that they have dark backs and dusky blotches on their pale bellies.
- Like other sharks in the Lamnidae family, salmon sharks are endothermic. They have an inbuilt heat exchanger that retains the heat generated by their metabolism and swimming muscles to keep them warm in frosty waters. This makes them smart and fast hunters.
- These wide-ranging sharks migrate over 27,000 km (16,800 miles) to feed and breed.

CONSERVATION STATUS

Least Concern

MAXIMUM SIZE

3 m (10 ft)

FIN FACT

Can keep its body temperature 21°C (70°F) warmer than the surrounding water.

BASKING SHARK

CETORHINUS MAXIMUS

HABITAT

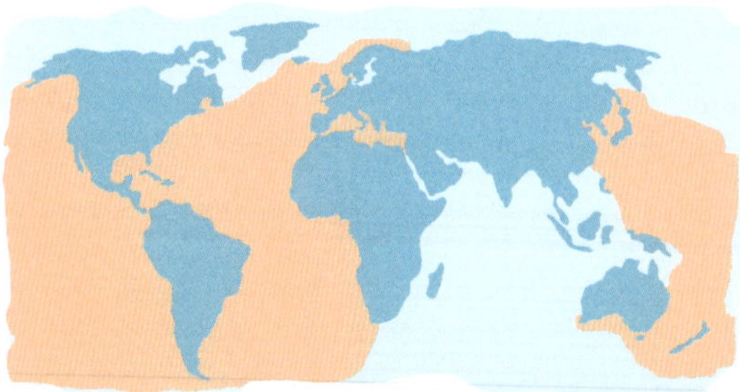

Basking sharks often swim slowly at the sea surface with their mouth open – their name comes from their habit of 'sunning' themselves. They prefer waters between 8°C and 16°C (46–61°F).

DIET

These sharks feed on zooplankton (small crustaceans, fish and invertebrate larvae, and fish eggs). They use their brush-like gill rakers to strain the tiny creatures from the sea water.

BIOLOGY

- The second-largest living fish in the ocean, basking sharks live up to 50 years and can weigh 6 tonnes (6.6 tons). They are so big that dolphins use them to swim faster with less effort (a trick known as bow-riding).
- Basking sharks are highly migratory, crossing oceans and moving between the Earth's hemispheres to find food.
- There's lots more to learn about basking sharks, but scientists think the females mature at 16 to 20 years old. After a three-year gestation, they give birth to about six large pups, each 1.5–2 m (5–6.5 ft) long. The mother then has a break of two to four years between litters.

CONSERVATION STATUS

Endangered

MAXIMUM SIZE

12 m (39 ft)

FIN FACT

Despite its huge size, it can leap out of the water – possibly to rid itself of parasites.

POCKET SHARK

MOLLISQUAMA SP.

HABITAT

Only two pocket sharks have ever been seen, but we know they are deep-dwelling sharks.

DIET

The diet of these extraordinary sharks is still a mystery.

BIOLOGY

- Pocket sharks (*Mollisquama parini*) are known from a single female shark 40 cm (16 in) long that was collected off the Chilean coast in the Pacific Ocean in 1984. Although this shark was caught at a depth of 330 m (1,080 ft), the ocean in this area is very deep, over 3,000 m (9,800 ft).
- More recently, in 2010, an immature male American pocket shark (*Mollisquama mississippiensis*) measuring 14 cm (5.5 in) long was found in the Gulf of Mexico in water over 3,000 m (9,800 ft) deep.
- Although they could easily fit in your pocket, these sharks are in fact named after the unique pocket-like glands above their **pectoral fins**.

CONSERVATION STATUS

Least Concern

MAXIMUM SIZE

40 cm (16 in)

FIN FACT

Produces a luminous liquid in special glands.

SMALLSPOTTED CATSHARK

SCYLIORHINUS CANICULA

HABITAT

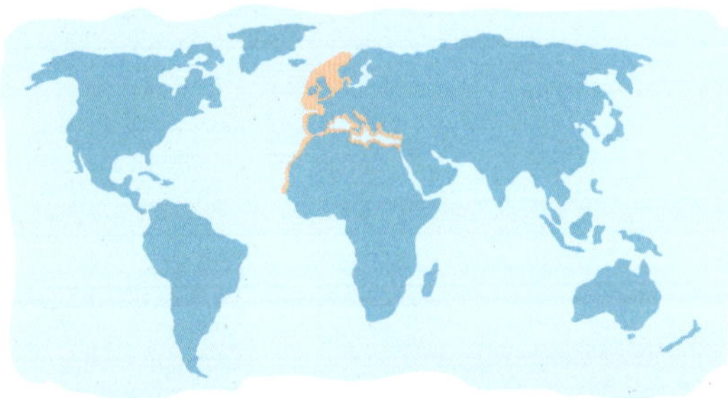

Smallspotted catsharks are found in the Atlantic Ocean, the North, Mediterranean and Black seas, and in European and North African coastal waters from 10 m to 80 m (33–262 ft) deep. They aren't too particular, sometimes occurring in midwater but also in a variety of habitats, including sandy, algal, gravel and muddy bottoms.

DIET

These nocturnal sharks feed on molluscs, crustaceans, worms, and small bony fish and cephalopods.

BIOLOGY

- Although catsharks are indeed generally small, they make up one of the largest families of sharks. Slender sharks with a short, rounded snout, these light grey or beige sharks are covered in small, well-defined, tightly spaced dark spots on the body and slightly larger, less concentrated spots on the fins.
- Females lay a pair of eggs in shallow areas. The egg cases have tendrils at each corner to anchor them to marine plants like seagrass.
- These catsharks have small **dermal denticles**, so their skin is not as rough as other sharks.

CONSERVATION STATUS

Least Concern

MAXIMUM SIZE

1 m (3 ft)

FIN FACT

Known in the past as the 'sea dog' because of their ferocious, pack-like feeding behaviour.

FRILLED SHARK

CHLAMYDOSELACHUS ANGUINEUS

HABITAT

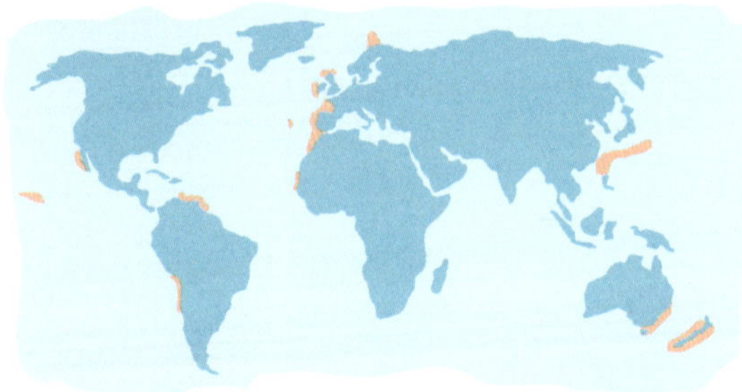

Frilled sharks dwell in waters 500–1,000 m (1,640–3,280 ft) deep, but they occasionally come to the surface. They have a wide-ranging but patchy distribution in the Atlantic and Pacific oceans.

DIET

They feed on squid, bony fish and other sharks. They have several rows of sharp but tiny teeth, each with three long points, that are perfect for snagging soft-bodied squid.

BIOLOGY

- Frilled sharks are strange, prehistoric-looking sharks with a long, cylindrical body. These snake- or eel-like sharks have six gill slits (most sharks have five). The lower ends of the first gill slits connect across the throat, forming the 'frill' or 'cloak' that gives these sharks their common name.
- As frilled sharks live in the deep, dark waters of the open ocean, much of their lives are a mystery. However, we think they may aggregate for mating – 34 frilled sharks (19 females and 15 males) were caught together near the Azores archipelago in the Atlantic Ocean.

CONSERVATION STATUS

Least Concern

MAXIMUM SIZE

2 m (6.5 ft)

FIN FACT

This shark swims like a serpent!

BONNETHEAD SHARK

SPHYRNA TIBURO

HABITAT

Bonnetheads are found in the western Atlantic Ocean from the USA to Brazil, and in the eastern Pacific Ocean from the USA to Ecuador. These social sharks are often found in groups of up to 15 individuals, called shivers.

DIET

These sharks feed during the day on crustaceans, such as crabs and shrimp, molluscs and small fish. They even burrow under coral heads to find fish and invertebrates to eat.

BIOLOGY

- Bonnetheads are the smallest of the nine species of hammerhead sharks, but the only species that has a shovel-shaped head. The front of its head is semicircular in outline.
- These sharks travel long distances every day, and prefer waters above 21°C (70°F). They are sensitive to the Earth's magnetic field and may use this to navigate during migration.
- These sharks are equipped with almost 360° vision and have excellent depth perception.

CONSERVATION STATUS

Endangered

MAXIMUM SIZE

1.5 m (5 ft)

FIN FACT

Sometimes eats seagrass, especially as a pup.

TIGER SHARK

GALEOCERDO CUVIER

HABITAT

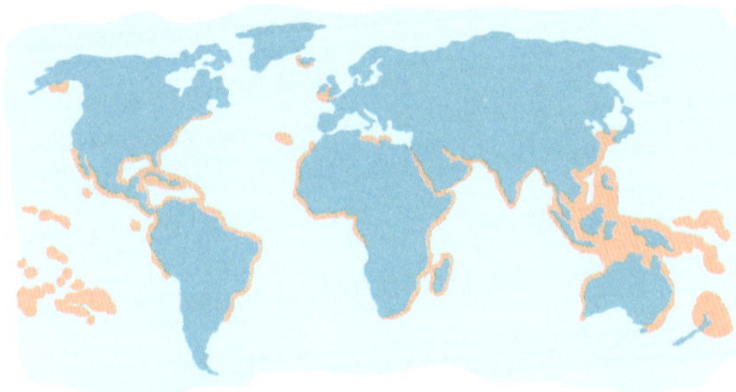

Tiger sharks live in tropical and warm temperate oceans (above 22°C or 72°F) worldwide, and seasonally follow warmer currents into cooler temperate waters.

DIET

Tiger sharks are nocturnal scavengers. They eat almost anything – garbage, metal, plastics, and even number plates from cars have been found in their stomachs. Smaller tiger sharks generally eat fish and invertebrates. As they grow bigger and older, they feed on sharks, rays and turtles.

BIOLOGY

- Tiger sharks are the fourth-largest shark. They have a short, bluntly rounded snout, large eyes and a slightly flattened head on a powerful, torpedo-shaped body.
- They can live for over 30 years. Females mature at 3.3 m (11 ft) long and males when at about 3 m (10 ft). Females give birth to a litter of up to 80 pups that are 51–104 cm (20–41 in) long.
- They are **lecithotrophic viviparous** – the developing embryos live completely off the yolk but are born alive and fully developed.

CONSERVATION STATUS

Near Threatened

MAXIMUM SIZE

7.5 m (25 ft)

FIN FACT

They are named after their tiger-like stripes that fade with age.

OCEANIC WHITETIP SHARK

CARCHARHINUS LONGIMANUS

HABITAT

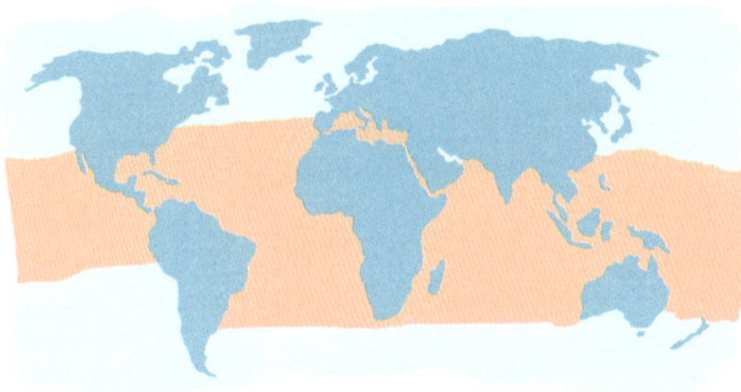

This shark swims across entire tropical and temperate oceans – usually far from land, although they sometimes come closer to shore. Although they prefer surface waters, oceanic whitetips also dive down to depths of 1,082 m (3,550 ft).

DIET

Meals are few and far between in the open ocean, so these opportunistic sharks feed on most things they encounter, including tuna, cephalopods, sharks, seabirds – even dead mammals and garbage.

BIOLOGY

- Oceanic whitetip sharks were once the most numerous **pelagic** sharks in tropical seas, but their numbers have declined by 98% worldwide. Easily recognised, these solitary sharks have white tips on their large rounded first **dorsal fin**, long paddle-like **pectoral fins** and **tail fins**.
- To breathe, these highly migratory sharks must keep moving to ensure water flows across their gills. They swim slowly, with their huge **pectoral fins** spread widely, often accompanied by remoras, dolphinfish and pilot fish.

CONSERVATION STATUS

Critically Endangered

MAXIMUM SIZE

3.5 m (11 ft)

FIN FACT

Oceanic whitetip sharks travel thousands of kilometres to breed!

ZEBRA SHARK

STEGOSTOMA TIGRINUM

HABITAT

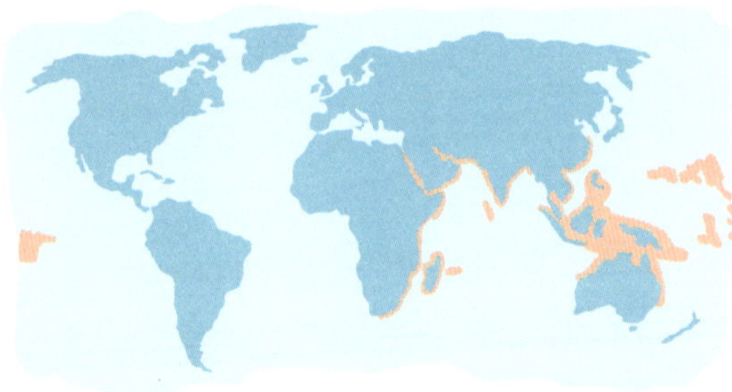

The zebra shark swims in tropical and subtropical inshore waters of the Indian and western Pacific oceans, and are usually found within shallow coral, rocky reefs and soft-bottomed sandy plateaus. They often rest on the bottom but also go to depths of 62 m (200 ft). They have even been recorded in fresh water!

DIET

Their flexible bodies allow them to squirm into reef channels and tight crevices to find small fish, sea snakes, gastropods and crustaceans.

BIOLOGY

- These beautiful coastal carpet sharks are named for the pups' banded black-and-white, zebra-like pattern. These zebras lose their stripes, eventually becoming yellow-brown spotty adults.
- Zebra sharks are **oviparous** and release 17 cm (7 in) dark brown or purplish black egg cases, which are then anchored to the sea floor with tufts of hair-like fibres.
- Travelling more than 2,000 km (1,250 miles) along the coast, zebra sharks show strong site fidelity to particular reefs in Australia and Thailand.

CONSERVATION STATUS

Endangered

MAXIMUM SIZE

3.5 m (11 ft)

FIN FACT

The female can reproduce asexually, meaning her pups are essentially clones!

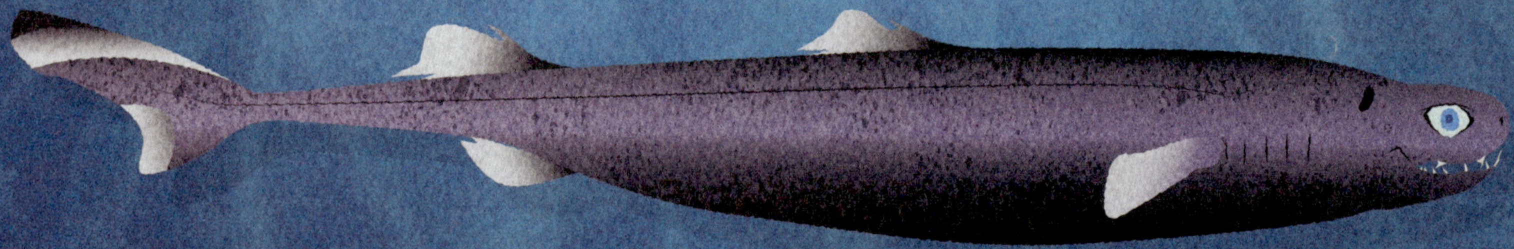

VIPER DOGFISH

TRIGONOGNATHUS KABEYAI

HABITAT

These rare sharks are **endemic** to the Pacific Ocean off Japan and Hawaii. As they occur in deep oceanic waters (250–1,000 m or 820–3,280 ft) and have been caught at night at a depth of 150 m (490 ft) in waters more than 1,500 m (4,900 ft) deep, they probably migrate vertically – moving towards the surface at night and retreating to the depths during the day.

DIET

This shark mainly eats lanternfish, crustaceans and cephalopods.

BIOLOGY

- As viper dogfish live in the deep, dark waters of the open ocean, their lives are a mystery. They are only known from about 56 specimens (55 from Japan and one from Hawaii).
- They use thousands of **ventral** photophores (hormonally controlled photogenic organs) to obliterate their silhouette in the water column, making them virtually invisible when viewed from below.
- Their triangular jaws have needle-like teeth that project forward to snap up elusive prey, similar to the goblin shark.

CONSERVATION STATUS

Least Concern

MAXIMUM SIZE

54 cm (21 in)

FIN FACT

Has translucent upper eyelids.

MEGALODON

OTODUS MEGALODON

HABITAT

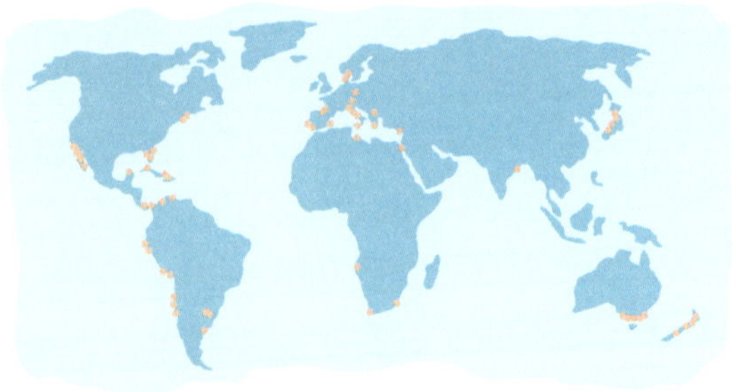

These highly migratory sharks lived in warm tropical and subtropical oceans worldwide. Megalodon teeth have been found on every continent, except Antarctica. The map above shows where fossil evidence of these giants have been found.

DIET

We know from their large, serrated teeth that megalodon were meat eaters that ate large prey such as whales, large fish and other sharks.

BIOLOGY

- Megalodon dominated the ocean between 23 and 2.6 million years ago. They were capable of swimming for a long time and used bursts of immense speed to catch prey.
- A 16 m (52 ft) megalodon had a 4.65 m (15 ft) head, a 1.62 m (5.3 ft) **dorsal fin** and a 3.85 m (13 ft) tail.
- Although we may never know for sure, we think megalodon became extinct as their prey numbers dwindled, temperatures changed and other marine predators arose.

CONSERVATION STATUS

Extinct

MAXIMUM SIZE

16 m (52 ft)

FIN FACT

Scientists have identified fossilised megalodon vertebrae the size of dinner plates.

BULL SHARK

HABITAT

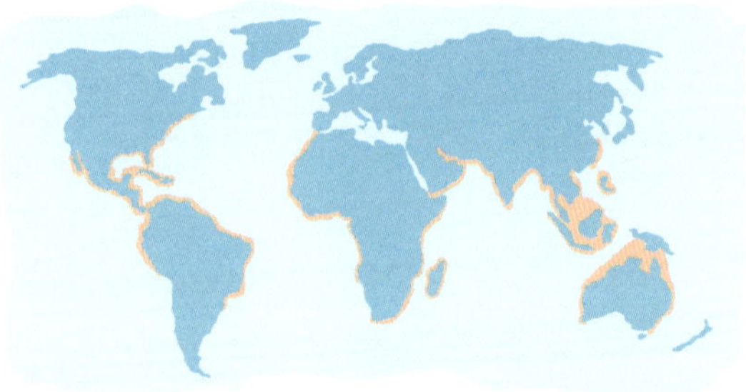

Bull sharks are widespread in tropical and subtropical oceans, rivers and lakes from the surf zone to a depth of 250 m (820 ft). They can stay in fresh water for a long time and have been found almost 4,000 km (2,500 miles) from the ocean in more than 120 freshwater rivers and lakes.

DIET

Bull sharks mainly prey on fish, but they will eat almost anything, including dolphins, stingrays, turtles, antelope, cattle, rats and other sharks.

BIOLOGY

- While most sharks have to live in the ocean to keep salt in their bodies, bull sharks have specially adapted to survive in fresh water. Females sometimes give birth in river mouths, where the young live for up to five years.
- Bull sharks undertake long-range migrations along coastlines. They can travel up to 180 km (110 miles) in 24 hours.
- They throw up indigestible food items, such as bones and turtle shell, that can't pass through the stomach. They hunt during the day and at night.

CONSERVATION STATUS

Vulnerable

MAXIMUM SIZE

4 m (13 ft)

FIN FACT

It can bite with the greatest force of any shark!

ANGELSHARK

SQUATINA SQUATINA

HABITAT

Angelsharks live on or near the sea floor in temperate waters 1–150 m (3–490 ft) deep. They are found in the north-eastern Atlantic Ocean, the Mediterranean Sea and the Black Sea.

DIET

Their diet consists of flatfish and other bottom-dwelling fish, but they will also eat skates, crustaceans, molluscs and even cormorants (a seabird).

BIOLOGY

- There are at least 23 species of angelsharks in the Squatinidae family. All have a flat body with long **pelvic** and **pectoral fins**. The skin has flecks of black, brown, grey, green and white.
- Their body shape and colour patterns provide camouflage when they lie buried in the sandy sea floor, perfectly still, with just their eyes exposed. Their **spiracles** act like a snorkel sticking out of the sand to deliver oxygen straight to the brain, allowing them to breathe while under the sand. Angelsharks are nocturnal ambush predators. They can lie in wait for days, then strike passing prey within one-tenth of a second.

CONSERVATION STATUS

Critically Endangered

MAXIMUM SIZE

2.4 m (8 ft)

FIN FACT

The common name comes from the angel's-wing shape of its fins.

SCALLOPED HAMMERHEAD SHARK

SPHYRNA LEWINI

HABITAT

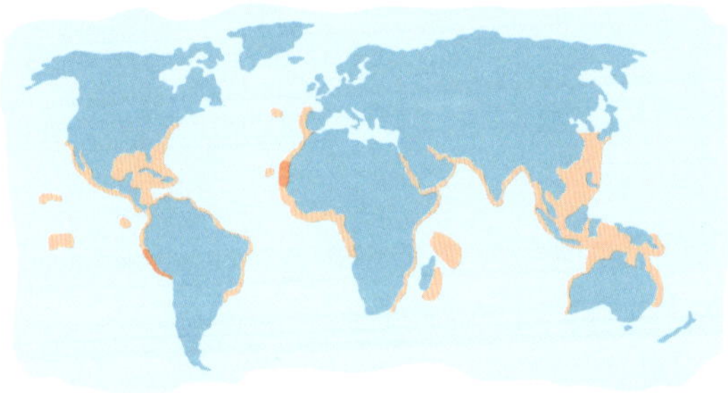

These sharks are coastal and semi-oceanic, living in warm, tropical and temperate waters. Although they are mostly found in the top 25 m (82 ft) of the ocean, they can dive to 1,000 m (3,280 ft).

DIET

They have relatively small mouths despite their large heads, which are equipped with sensitive **ampullae of Lorenzini**, to help them find prey buried in the sand. They mainly eat bony fish, smaller sharks and rays, squid, octopus and crustaceans.

BIOLOGY

- Scalloped hammerhead sharks have a cephalofoil – a wide head shaped like a double-ended hammer, with eyes on each end. Their arched head has an indentation front and centre, with two more either side of the main one that give them a scalloped appearance.
- Females mature at 13 years of age and can live for 35 years.
- Juveniles are found in large schools, while adults travel alone, in pairs or in schools. Scalloped hammerheads are both residents and travellers – some live permanently in one area, while other, smaller individuals form huge schools and migrate towards the poles in summer.

CONSERVATION STATUS

Critically Endangered

MAXIMUM SIZE

4.3 m (14 ft)

FIN FACT

When diving deep into cold waters, they hold their breath to keep themselves warm!

SILKY SHARK

CARCHARHINUS FALCIFORMIS

HABITAT

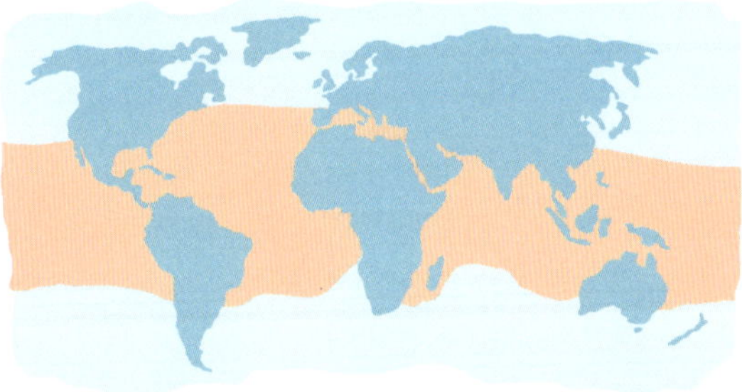

Silky sharks are both coastal and oceanic in tropical waters globally. They range from living near the surface to depths of at least 500 m (1,640 ft), and often swim near islands, slopes and over deepwater reefs in waters around 23°C (73°F).

DIET

The diet of these speedy sharks consists of fish, squid, paper nautiluses and crabs.

BIOLOGY

- Silky sharks have a long, rounded, flat snout, small jaws and large eyes. Their slim bodies are grey to bluish grey on top, and pale underneath, without conspicuous markings on the fins.
- Smaller silky sharks inhabit coastal nurseries while adults venture further offshore over deeper water. Adolescent silky sharks leave their nursery grounds for offshore oceanic waters and frequently join tuna schools, to get some food on the run.
- Silky sharks are often seen near drifting materials on the surface of the open ocean. They are the second most caught shark after the blue shark.

CONSERVATION STATUS

Vulnerable

MAXIMUM SIZE

3.5 m (11 ft)

FIN FACT

This shark's common name comes from the silky look of their skin.

DAGGERNOSE SHARK

ISOGOMPHODON OXYRHYNCHUS

HABITAT

Daggernose sharks dwell in shallow waters (4–40 m or 13–131 ft) that are murky due to the drainage of the Amazonian estuary. Although mostly found in estuaries, river mouths and mangrove coastlines, they also venture into fresh water.

DIET

As these sharks have small eyes and a long snout and live in murky waters, they may rely on their **ampullae of Lorenzini** to detect the heartbeat of their prey, which are probably schooling fish.

BIOLOGY

- As the name implies, these sharks have a distinctive long and prominent snout with very large, paddle-shaped **pectoral fins**. These fins originate behind the head and extend outwards, providing lift and allowing the sharks to steer while they are swimming.
- Females live to 20 years of age, but males only to 12 years of age. Females are thought to give birth every second year, to three to seven pups.
- Like all sharks, a daggernose shark's skeleton is made of cartilage – just like our noses and ears.

CONSERVATION STATUS

Critically Endangered

MAXIMUM SIZE

1.6 m (5 ft)

FIN FACT

Has one of the smallest ranges of any living shark and all individuals belong to one population.

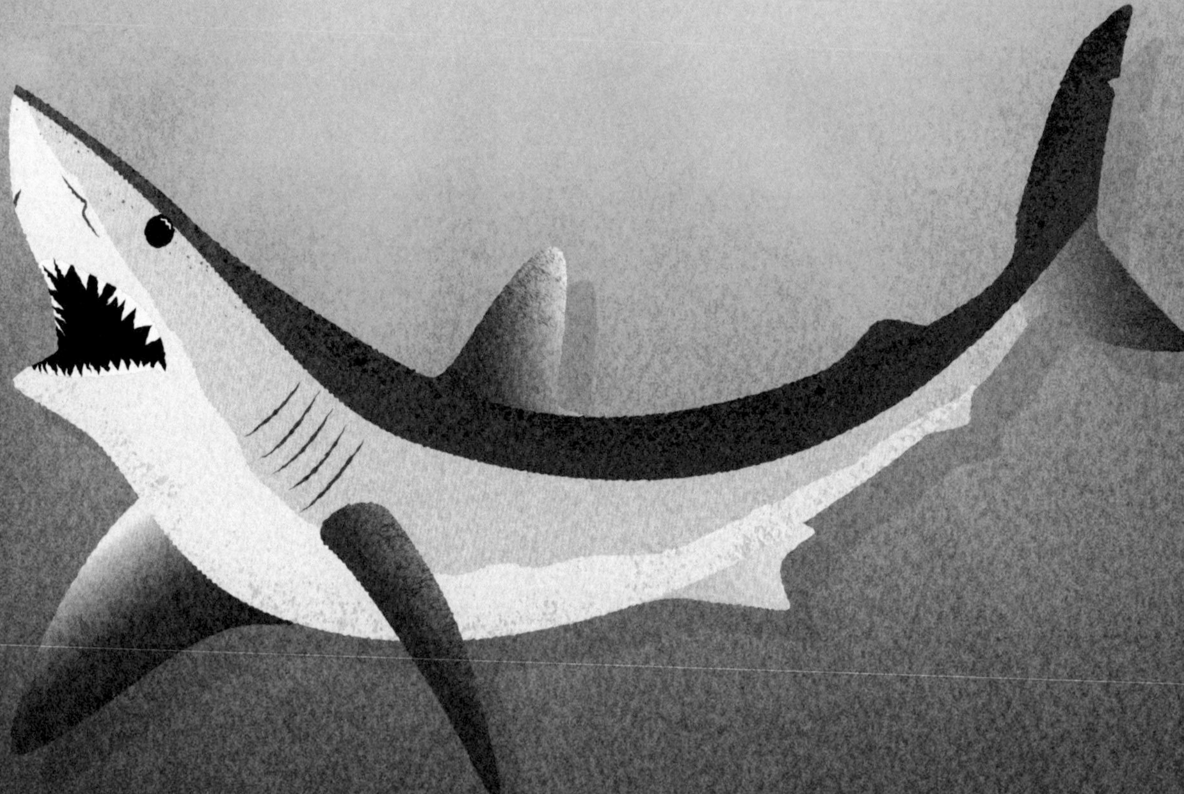

SHORTFIN MAKO SHARK

ISURUS OXYRINCHUS

HABITAT

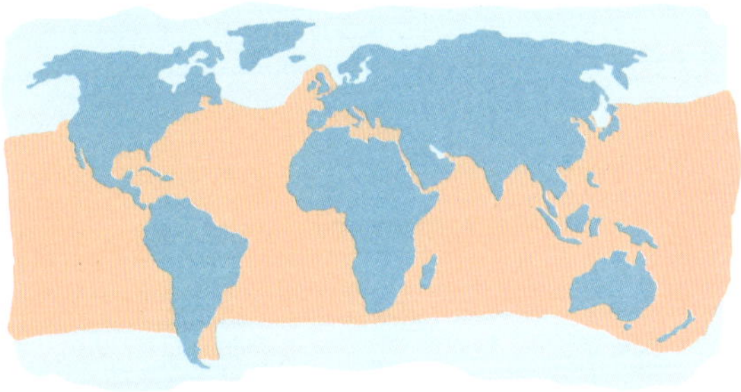

Shortfin mako sharks are highly migratory and occur worldwide in waters above 16°C (61°F). They live in the open ocean to depths of 888 m (2,910 ft) but are usually found in the top 150 m (490 ft). They sometimes come close to the shore too.

DIET

Makos eat a variety of prey, such as fish (including other sharks), squid and turtles. When they mature at over 3 m (10 ft) long they prey on larger billfish, such as marlin and sailfish, and small marine mammals.

BIOLOGY

- There are two species of mako sharks – the shortfin and longfin. The longfin mako shark (*Isurus paucus*) is a poorly known **pelagic** species that have slimmer bodies and longer **pectoral fins** when compared to the shortfin.
- Mako sharks are special. Like other sharks in the Lamnidae family, they have a heat exchange circulatory system that keeps their bodies warmer than the surrounding water. This allows them to stay very active and they can even leap out of the water!

CONSERVATION STATUS

Endangered

MAXIMUM SIZE

4.4 m (14 ft)

FIN FACT

Swim at speeds of up to 74 km/h (46 mph), making it the fastest shark in the ocean!

GHOST SHARK

CALLORHINCHUS MILII

HABITAT

Ghost sharks are found in the Pacific Ocean of southern Australia and New Zealand to depths of 227 m (745 ft).

DIET

These silvery white fish mainly eat invertebrates and shellfish.

BIOLOGY

- This unusual fish is a chimaera – not a true shark, but a relative that also swapped bones for cartilage.
- Ghost sharks have a long spine located in front of their first **dorsal fin** for defence. They also have a small, club-like, protruding snout highly sensitive to electric fields that they use to search for snacks.
- Ghost sharks live for 9 to 20 years and every year the females lay about 20 eggs that are encased in horny shells.

CONSERVATION STATUS

Least Concern

MAXIMUM SIZE

1.2 m (4 ft)

FIN FACT

Ghost shark's eyes have reflective tissue that seem to glow eerily in the dark.

GREY NURSE SHARK

CARCHARIAS TAURUS

HABITAT

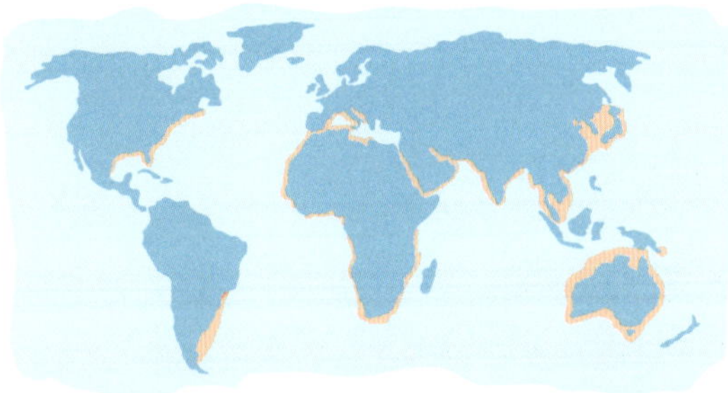

Grey nurse sharks live near land in the Atlantic, Indian and western Pacific oceans. They are mainly found in groups in shallow waters from 15 m to 25 m (49–82 ft) deep. They prefer to be in or near underwater caves, deep sandy gullies and reefs.

DIET

They prey on bony fish, small sharks, rays, squid and lobsters.

BIOLOGY

- Also known as sand tiger sharks, grey nurse sharks have a large, stout body that is dark grey to greyish brown above and off-white underneath. The scattered brownish or reddish blotches on the rear of their bodies fade as they get older – and can be used to identify individuals. They are slow but strong swimmers that are most active at night.
- Grey nurse sharks are **ovoviviparous**. After the largest embryos have absorbed their yolk sac, they feed on other eggs then cannibalise their smaller unborn siblings. Only two embryos survive – one from each uterus. They are both quite large, about 1 m (3 ft) in length and at birth are already experienced hunters.

CONSERVATION STATUS

Critically Endangered

MAXIMUM SIZE

3.3 m (11 ft)

FIN FACT

Stays buoyant by swallowing air and holding it in its stomach!

MEGAMOUTH SHARK

MEGACHASMA PELAGIOS

HABITAT

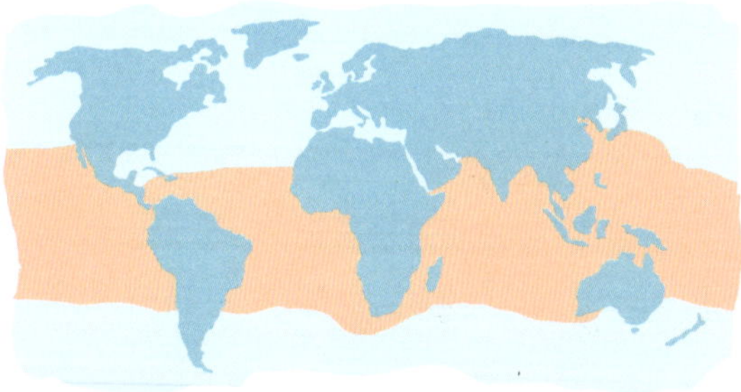

Although it is not clear exactly where they live, these mysterious sharks are thought to be wide-ranging in tropical and temperate areas of all major oceans. They are mostly seen off the coasts of China, Japan and the Philippines.

DIET

Megamouths are thought to follow the daily vertical migrations of their zooplankton prey such as shrimp, copepods and sea jellies, swimming to the surface at night and in the ocean depths during the day.

BIOLOGY

- This shark has possibly the most amazing scientific name of any species: *Megachasma pelagios*, meaning 'giant mouth of the deep sea'. It is a fitting name, as the mouth on a 5 m (16 ft) megamouth shark is about 1.3 m (4 ft) wide.
- Megamouth sharks have an unusual white band hidden in a groove that is only visible when the jaw is open. Its purpose is unknown – it could be a unique fingerprint, a glowing lure or used to reflect glowing prey.
- These rarely observed sharks fall victim to the semi-parasitic cookiecutter shark.
- Megamouths are the smallest of the three filter-feeding sharks (after whale sharks and basking sharks).

CONSERVATION STATUS

Least Concern

MAXIMUM SIZE

5.5 m (18 ft)

FIN FACT

This species was discovered in 1983 when one was found tangled in a sea anchor.

EPAULETTE SHARK

HEMISCYLLIUM OCELLATUM

HABITAT

Epaulette sharks are commonly found in shallow coastal waters in northern Australia and New Guinea.

DIET

These little sharks are most active at low tide and at night, particularly around sunrise and sunset, hunting crustaceans, worms and small fish.

BIOLOGY

- Epaulette sharks can survive in low-oxygen (hypoxic) conditions by switching off their non-essential brain functions. This comes in handy when they hunt barely submerged in warm, shallow, oxygen-depleted rock pools.
- Female epaulette sharks lay a pair of eggs and hide them in coral at night. They can produce a pair of egg capsules every 14 days and the embryos feed on their yolk.
- Before copulation, the male grasps the female by biting her body and even her gills.

CONSERVATION STATUS

Least Concern

MAXIMUM SIZE

1.1 m (3.5 ft)

FIN FACT

Uses its muscular fins to 'walk' between rock pools as it forages for food!

SPINY DOGFISH

SQUALUS ACANTHIAS

HABITAT

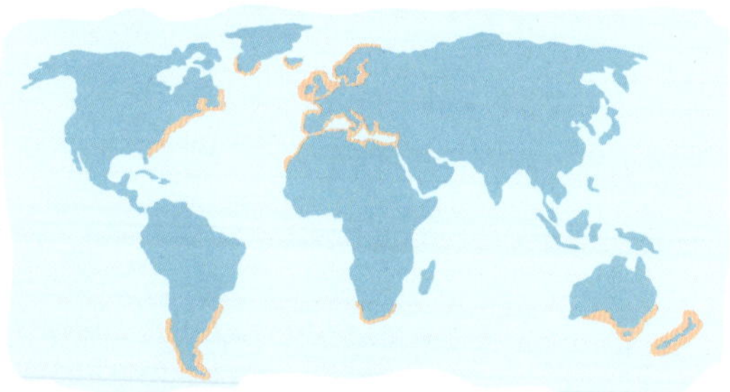

These migratory sharks swim from the surface down to almost 2,000 m (6,600 ft), but are usually found between 50 m and 300 m (164–980 ft). Spiny dogfish have a global distribution in the Atlantic, Indian and Pacific oceans (but not in the north Pacific Ocean) as well as in the Mediterranean and Black seas.

DIET

They feed on a wide variety of prey, ranging from comb jellyfish, squid, mackerel and herring to shrimp, crabs and even sea cucumbers.

BIOLOGY

- These long, slender sharks are a brownish slate colour with a pale underbelly and rows of white spots. They also have large eyes and a pointed snout.
- Be careful if you encounter one as spiny dogfish have spines in front of both **dorsal fins** and can inflict toxins with their tail.
- These schooling sharks can live for 30 years and size matters – larger, older females produce bigger pups in larger litters that are more likely to survive than the pups of smaller mothers.

CONSERVATION STATUS

Vulnerable

MAXIMUM SIZE

1.6 m (5 ft)

FIN FACT

These are possibly the most numerous shark alive in the ocean.

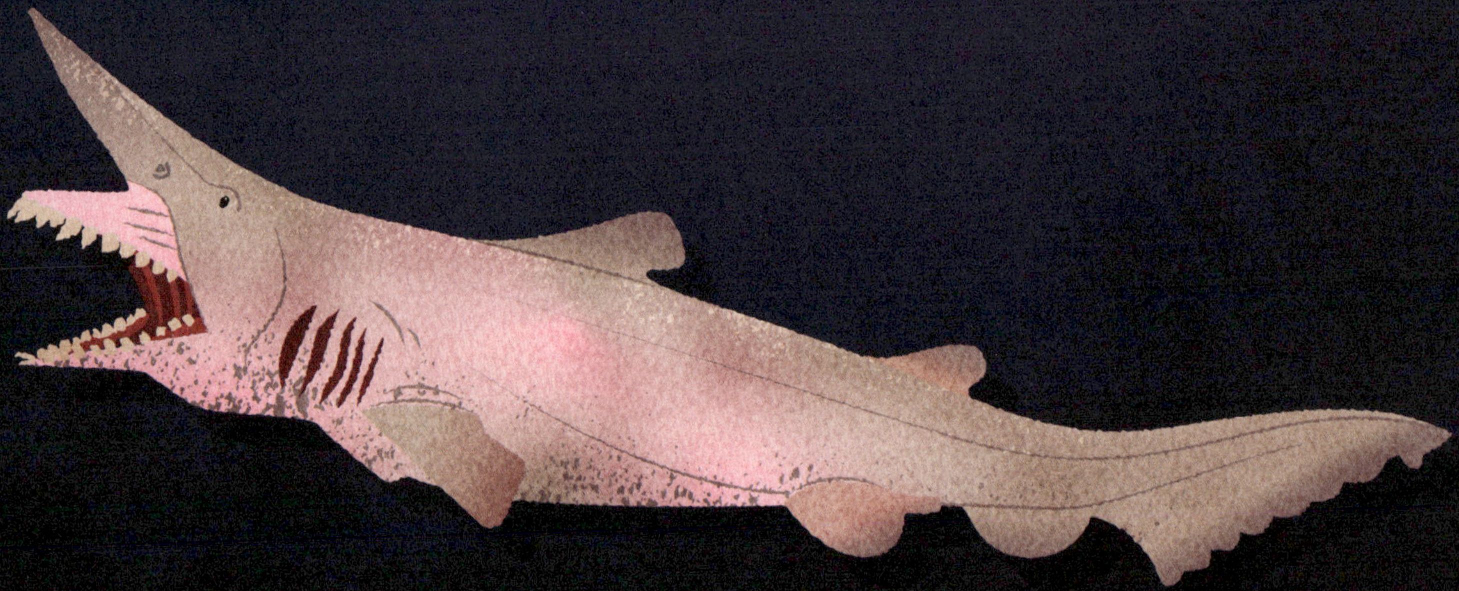

GOBLIN SHARK

MITSUKURINA OWSTONI

HABITAT

Goblin sharks have a widespread but patchy global distribution in the Atlantic, Indian and Pacific oceans. Most have been seen in waters ranging from 270 to 960 m (890–3,150 ft) deep, with the deepest found at 1,300 m (4,300 ft). The Pacific Ocean off Japan seems to be a hotspot for these sharks, but they are likely to be found in other areas not yet explored.

DIET

Goblin sharks prey on bony fish, squid, octopus and crustaceans.

BIOLOGY

- Not a lot is known about the biology of these deep-sea sharks.
- They are pinkish white (because their blood vessels are visible through the skin), and have bluish fins on flabby but slender bodies.
- Their most famous feature is their very long cusped teeth in long, protrusible jaws. The mouth retracts under the eyes and extends from beneath the flat, bladelike, long snout. They also have tiny eyes.
- When feeding, goblin sharks extend their jaws forward in a motion called 'slingshot feeding'.

CONSERVATION STATUS

Least Concern

MAXIMUM SIZE

6.2 m (20 ft)

FIN FACT

Can fire its jaws out of its head at high speeds to engulf nearby prey!

BLUE SHARK

PRIONACE GLAUCA

HABITAT

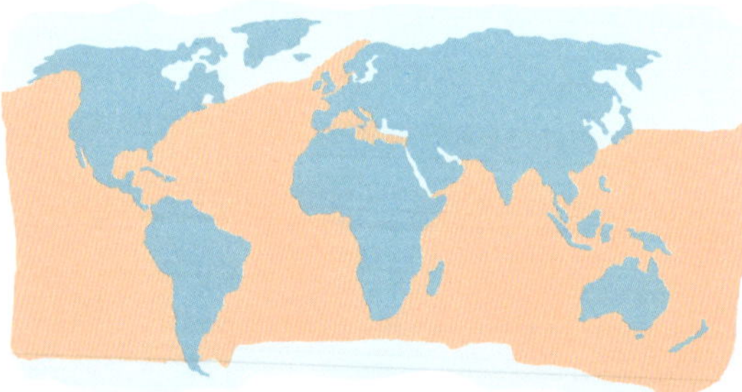

Blue sharks are one of the world's most wide-ranging sharks and prefer waters of 12–20°C (54–68°F). They swim in the tropical and temperate waters of all oceans and are found in open-ocean (**pelagic**) waters to a depth of 1,000 m (3,280 ft).

DIET

Blue sharks are swift predators that feed on bony fish, squid and marine mammals.

BIOLOGY

- These eye-catching sharks have a very distinctive bright blue body. Their **countershading**, dark blue (almost indigo) **dorsal** surface, lighter blue flanks and abruptly white bellies make them nearly invisible when viewed from above or below.
- Blue sharks are one of the most caught sharks in the world. Because they swim great distances and cross oceans – one has travelled more than 28,000 km (17,400 miles) in 2.6 years – we consider them to be a single population.
- They mature young and can have up to 135 pups in each litter (depending on the mother's size).

CONSERVATION STATUS

Near Threatened

MAXIMUM SIZE

4 m (13 ft)

FIN FACT

The females' skin is three times thicker than the skin of the males.

SOUTHERN SAWSHARK

PRISTIOPHORUS NUDIPINNIS

HABITAT

Southern sawsharks are **endemic** to southern Australia. They can swim down to depths of 600 m (1,970 ft) but mostly swim in the top 80 m (260 ft).

DIET

Sawsharks prey on small fish, molluscs and crustaceans.

BIOLOGY

- Sawsharks are easily identified by their distinctive tapered saw-like blade (rostrum) that has alternating long and short 'teeth' on the edges. This toothed rostrum is used to sense, capture and manipulate prey. Paired elongated feelers underneath the rostrum also help them detect a snack.
- There are 10 species of sawshark and all have a large **spiracle** behind each eye to breathe while lying on the sea floor.
- The long rostral teeth are folded back when the sawshark is born, no doubt making it easier on the mother. Smaller teeth grow in between the larger ones as the pup grows, and sawteeth are replaced and added when there is space available on the rostrum.

CONSERVATION STATUS

Least Concern

MAXIMUM SIZE

1.2 m (4 ft)

FIN FACT

Females can produce pups from several fathers in the same litter!

PONDICHERRY SHARK

CARCHARHINUS HEMIODON

HABITAT

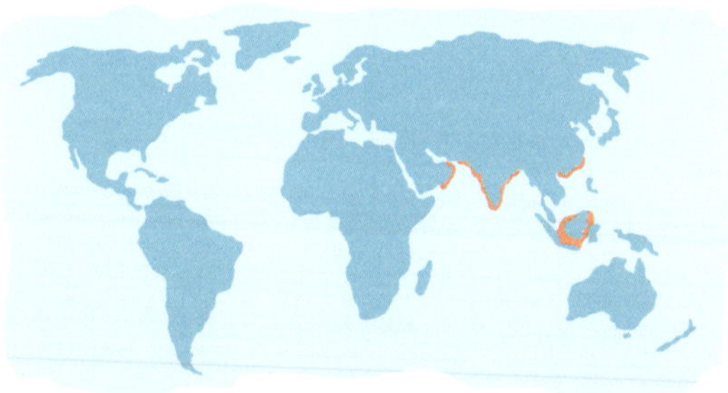

Pondicherry sharks were historically thought to live from Oman on the Arabian Sea to the South China Sea and Borneo, but this is based on only a few sharks caught across a large area. There are more recent records, including reported sightings in rivers, but as these are unverified this species remains a mystery.

DIET

Although the diet of these cryptic carcharhinids is unknown, they probably prey on small fish, crustaceans and cephalopods.

BIOLOGY

- Pondicherry sharks are grey above and white beneath, with black tips on the **caudal** and **pectoral** fins. The other fins are dusky coloured.
- We only know of this shark from fewer than 20 museum specimens that are more than 60 years old.
- The biology of this very rare shark is unknown; however, it belongs to the well-studied group of requiem sharks in the Carcharhinidae family. Like other requiem sharks, they have five pairs of gills on the side of their head and they need to keep oxygenated water flowing over their gills to breathe.

CONSERVATION STATUS

Critically Endangered

MAXIMUM SIZE

1.2 m (4 ft)

FIN FACT

There are only about 249 mature Pondicherry sharks in the world.

GANGES SHARK

GLYPHIS GANGETICUS

HABITAT

These elusive sharks have a patchy distribution from Pakistan and India to Myanmar and Borneo. Although specialised to live in large rivers and estuaries, they also rely on marine environments. Juveniles and adolescents live in rivers, and move to marine and coastal waters when they mature.

DIET

The diet of these cryptic sharks is unknown, but their sharp slender teeth suggest that fish make up a large part of their diet.

BIOLOGY

- The Ganges shark is one of four, or maybe five, species of river shark, along with the Borneo River shark and Irrawaddy River shark. As records of this rare river shark are mostly old and often based on only their jaws, we only know a little about them.
- Ganges sharks have a stocky grey-brown body, broadly rounded snout and small eyes.
- The fact that their small eyes tilt **dorsally** (towards the top) tells us a lot. These sharks probably inhabit cloudy, muddy water with limited visibility, and swim along the bottom, scanning the waters above for potential prey that is more easily seen when backlit by the sun.

CONSERVATION STATUS

Critically Endangered

MAXIMUM SIZE

2.8 m (9 ft)

FIN FACT

May travel thousands of kilometres to breed.

ORNATE WOBBEGONG

ORECTOLOBUS ORNATUS

HABITAT

Found in the western Pacific Ocean (near Indonesia, Papua New Guinea and Australia), ornate wobbegongs spend their days resting in caves or under ledges, and prefer sponge gardens and barren boulders. They can be found in coastal reefs to depths of at least 100 m (330 ft) and are homebodies that stay in the same place for a while.

DIET

At night, these ambush predators dine on small fish and crustaceans.

BIOLOGY

- Of the 11 known species of wobbegongs, 10 live in Australian waters. There may even be other, undescribed, species, from Papua New Guinea, Indonesia and Japan.
- Despite their wild appearance, ornate wobbegong sharks are excellently camouflaged against their surroundings and are relatively docile.
- Wobbegongs have a very large **spiracle** behind each eye, which they use for breathing when they are resting.

CONSERVATION STATUS

Least Concern

MAXIMUM SIZE

1.2 m (4 ft)

FIN FACT

Named for its ornate patterns and bearded jaws – 'wobbegong' means 'shaggy beard'.

Published in 2026 by Little Smith,
an imprint of Smith Street Books
Naarm (Melbourne) | Australia
smithstreetbooks.com

Distributed outside of ANZ, North & Latin America by
Thames & Hudson Ltd., 6–24 Britannia Street, London, WC1X 9JD
thamesandhudson.com

EU Authorised Representative: Interart S.A.R.L.
19 rue Charles Auray, 93500 Pantin, Paris, France
productsafety@thameshudson.co.uk; www.interart.fr

ISBN: 978-1-9235-0328-1

Smith Street Books respectfully acknowledges the Wurundjeri People of the Kulin Nation, who are the Traditional Owners of the land on which we work, and we pay our respects to their Elders past and present.

Series publisher: Hannah Koelmeyer
Commissioning editor: Aisling Coughlan
Design concept: Kristy Lund-White
Design layout: Nikola Roberts
Proofreader: Pamela Dunne
Production manager: Aisling Coughlan

Printed & bound in China by
C&C Offset Printing Co., Ltd.

Book 466
10 9 8 7 6 5 4 3 2 1

FSC
www.fsc.org
MIX
Paper | Supporting responsible forestry
FSC® C008047

Dr Charlotte Birkmanis

is an award-winning marine biologist, wildlife science presenter, professional speaker and ocean explorer who shares the secrets of the sea with kids and families around the world. You might have seen or heard her on the BBC and ABC, or read about her in *Forbes* magazine.

Dr Charlotte has visited more than 50 countries and lives in Queensland, Australia, where she studies sharks and other large fish, and partners with philanthropists who want to leave a legacy of thriving oceans for future generations. When she is not diving with sharks or sharing fun facts in English and Mandarin Chinese, she's creating talks, books and games to inspire everyone to help care for our blue planet.